HOW TO SURVIVE YOUR PARENTS' DIVORCE:

KIDS' ADVICE TO KIDS

Gayle Kimball, Ph.D.

Equality=Press

READERS' REACTIONS

"Uses words that little kids in third grade wouldn't understand, otherwise helpful and a great book."
> –Andrea, 12.

"Good hints about keeping equal love from your parents."
> –John, 14.

"This book gives people going through their parents' divorce an easier time."
> –Sadasa, 14.

"This book helps you understand your parents' divorce and you can understand what your friends go through."
> –Nicole, 14.

"Easy to read but says a lot. People 12 and up can benefit from it, including parents."
> –David, 18.

"It really helps to hear from other kids going through the same experience, then you don't feel so isolated by the divorce."
> – Jessica, 20.

"This book helped me to re-think my parents' divorce and learn important new concepts. An excellent book for kids, their parents, and even adults like myself."
> –Jennifer, 22.

"Full of great advice for kids, and parents too. In many ways, it's a peer support group in print."

> –Elizabeth McGonagle, school social worker,
> founder of Banana Splits, NY.

"I wish I'd had this book eight years ago when I divorced, to have insight into how my children would react then and in the future."

> –Pat Hanson, Ph.D., president of Health Matters, CA.

"This book is especially helpful as it speaks directly to the adolescents."

> –Julie Jacobson, director of Divorce Lifeline, WA.

"An outstanding and much needed resource for kids going through a divorce. Also for teachers, counselors, and parents. I loved it."

> –Sue Klavans Simring, D.S.W., Co-Director, Family
> Solutions, NJ.

"A wonderful list of techniques, especially about helping kids (and adults) be more verbal. A useful description of the normal processes and response to change."

> –Judy Osborne, Stepfamily Associates, MA.

"Practical, clear, and comprehensive guide. It can be reassuring for kids to know that strong feelings at this time are natural."

> –Lynne Reyman, counselor, CA.

"Has all the components I would recommend for dealing comprehensively with the issue of divorce."

> –Ellen VanDyken, school social worker, MI.

"A needed resource, full of excellent ideas to use in my kids' support group to provoke discussions. Especially good quotes from kids and journaling suggestions."

–Tony Nethercott, school counselor, MI.

"A great book of ideas, written from the expertise of kids who've experienced divorce. One of a kind."

–Linda Sartori, teacher and
editor of *Kids' Express* newsletter, CO.

"Divorce is an adult decision that often leaves the child emotionally wounded. This book offers the child tools for working through the process of emotional healing."

–Brian Holderman, teacher, leader of church
workshops for children of divorce, CA.

"This book inspired me, as a family mediator, to provide more support for the children of my divorcing clients. And it gives me an important tool which I can give the children to help themselves."

–Jon Luvaas, Mediator and Attorney, CA.

"Kids talking to kids about the ways they coped with and survived their parents' divorce is a terrific concept. A wonderful book that can help many children and their parents. The book gives practical and helpful advice that provides children of divorce the emotional help and hope they deserve."

–David. L. Levy, President, and Deborah Chad, student
intern, Children's Rights Council, Washington, D.C.

"In this very readable book, Dr. Kimball provides the facts about parental divorce to kids from kids. Content, language, and style make this an important book for young people from 12 to 18."

–Judith L. Bauersfeld, Ph.D., past president, Stepfamily Association of America, AZ.

Library of Congress Catalog Card Number #93-090844

Divorce/Children of Divorce.   For ages 12-18 and their parents.

Summary: 268 young people share how they coped with their parents' divorce. Includes comments from 20 counselors who work with youth whose parents are divorcing, illustrations, bibliography and resource lists.

ISBN 0-938795-22-8

Printed in the United States of America on recycled paper.

Other Books by the Author

Everything You Need to Know to Succeed After College, ed.
50/50 Parenting
50/50 Marriage
Women's Culture, ed

CONTENTS

AND:

Thanks to:

*my California State University, Chico, students for distributing questionnaires to their friends, completing questionnaires if their parents divorced, and criticizing drafts of this book.

*the Children's Rights Council in Washington, D.C. for their help in getting the word out to young people to fill out questionnaires and to Deborah Chad and David Levy for critiquing a draft.

*Stephanie Marshall's ninth grade class for adding their comments to a draft.

*mediator Jon Luvaas and his son Brent, lawyer Les Hait, and educator Billie Jackson for sharing their expertise.

*therapists Ro Bolen (San Francisco), Julie Jacobson and other Divorce Line therapists (Seattle), Grace Lucido (Chico, CA), Elizabeth McGonagle (Ballston Spa, NY), Tony Nethercott (Holland, MI), Judy Osborne (Boston), Lynne Reyman (Chico), Linda VanDyken (Holland, MI); professor Dolores Blalock (Chico), writer Lee Hirschbein (Chico), educator Pat Hanson (Paradise, CA), teacher Brian Holderman (Chico), and *Kids Express* editor Linda Sartori (Littleton, CO) for their written comments on a draft. Kids' group leaders Gwen Guillet (Del Mar, NY), Laurie Olbrish (Chicago), Susan March (Holland, MI), and Ann Marie Simmons (Irvine, CA) gave information over the phone, as did Shelly Schreier and Neil Kalter at the University of Michigan's Family Styles Project, Judith Bauersfeld–Stepfamily Association of America (AZ), stepfamily group leader Wendy Geis-Rockwood (Santa Barbara, CA), Anne Giel (Chico) and counselor Steve Flowers (Chico).

*Wendy Hoffman and Marilyn Nicokiris for tracking down library articles and books.

The Talent:

Cover and print design: Joseph E. Martin.

Drawings by eleventh and twelfth grade students in the order seen in the book: Onnah Sisk, Karisha Longaker, Anthony Morano, Annie Tullius, Nadia Puri, Stacey Vigallon, Casey Fay, Travis Crawford, and Walker Lee. Copy editors: Phyllis Mannion, Melissa Mead, and Pat Keyes Loder.

Photographer: Jeff Teeter.

Greetings

Your parents' divorce can be the most difficult and painful experience you will have as you grow up, especially if it separates you from one of your parents. Each year about one million young people go through their parents' divorce, so you're part of a large group. More than one-half of American youth will live in a single-parent family before they are 18: Ninety percent of these families are headed by a mother. Contact with fathers is likely to decrease after divorce, creating a major problem for kids.

Learning from other youths can make coping with divorce easier. Most divorce books for youth are geared for very young children and the few books that tell about kid's experiences in their own words are from the early eighties. Seeing a need for a book for the nineties, I asked 268 young people (ages 9 to 24) to write answers to 20 questions about divorce and did follow-up interviews with five of them. Then I asked 20 counselors, most of whom work with groups of kids of divorce, to add their comments and summarize the issues they hear from youth.

Forty-one percent of the youth are male and 59 percent are female. I had better luck getting girls to fill out questionnaires. (Throughout this book, I'll refer to the youth advising you as our "experts.") In a nutshell, what they say is that divorce is awful for those old enough to remember it, but it gets better with time if they have the loving support of their parents. The unhappy ones are kids whose parents turn their attention to work, dating, and remarriage, leaving their children feeling abandoned.

Why do I care about helping you through your family's change? Because my family went through it when my son Jed was only one year old. He's 14 now, but there are still times when he wishes his parents lived in the same house. He misses mom when he's at dad's and misses dad when he's at mom's. Friends can't keep track of where he is, and his karate *gi* and textbooks are at one house when they should be at the other. He likes having double holiday celebrations, gifts, vacations, rooms and pets, however! His advice to you is, "Have a say in what goes on." Mine is stay in touch with your feelings, even if they're uncomfortable, and let people know what you need to be your best.

My books for parents are *50/50 Marriage* and *50/50 Parenting*. The second book includes chapters on divorce and stepparenting. (A group effort I edited with 14 authors, titled *Everything You Need to Know to Succeed After College,* may be useful to you in the future.)

I was inspired to collect kids' advice about divorce by one of my college students who wrote a research paper describing how painful her parents' divorce was for her and her brothers. Unable to cope, she developed bulimia, an eating disorder, and other problems. Seeing her unhappiness made me want to do something to prevent this happening to others. I thought the best help would be from those who've been through divorce. The youth we interviewed for *50/50 Parenting* came up with the same conclusions as adult experts, causing me to respect young people's observations.

I asked my students and three national newsletters to send out questionnaires and then summarized the results for you to compare with your experiences. The typical experts are California college students in their early twenties, who experienced divorce before they were ten. But experts also include kids from elementary school on up, in states ranging from Ohio to New York. A ninth grade class and some of my college students added their comments to a draft of the book, as did counselors and other professionals who work with divorce.

My guess is your feelings are similar to other kids' and you will be glad to know your reactions are normal, even if you're angry and/ or sad. I strongly suggest you get a notebook or diary and start keeping a journal as you read. I have included questions for you to respond to (look for the 🐾) and put additional journal questions at the end of the book. When you read a list of quotations from our experts, marked by a 🐾, select the one that is closest to your experience. You may also respond to the high school students' drawings which begin each chapter.

Also included are techniques to help you carry out the advice of our experts, which you'll see outlined in the "How to...🐾" boxes. Jayce (21) and Chris (12) start each chapter by sharing their experiences with divorce.

Reading this book may bring up the unpleasant feelings that usually accompany

How to Keep a Journal

🐾 You might want to buy a locked journal or write in a notebook that looks dull and unimportant to anyone who might think about reading it. Get a pen or pencil you enjoy using. Don't be concerned about your handwriting or neatness, and be sure to hide it in a safe place. Give yourself permission to write anything that pops into your mind. Don't think, just write, as our experts agree that this activity really helps to sort out feelings and thoughts. You might want to include drawings, photos, quotes, and little souvenirs you like or that remind you of something pleasant. Make your journal a place you can go to cheer yourself up as well as to dump unhappy feelings.

This is an example of the the "How to..." headline and pawprint in this book.

the breakup of a family. The only way to heal, though, is to clean out the wound. This emotional work must be done now so it doesn't haunt you later, like a ghost. Gina, a college student, says, "If you deny the feelings you have from your parents' divorce, years later you may be affected by these hidden feelings. It's hard to realize where these feelings of anger, hurt, and distrust come from."

As you use this book, it's helpful to work with someone you trust, who is neutral and not emotionally involved with you. When we confront our deep feelings, we usually need someone who is not connected to us to give balance and perspective. Otherwise we can get swamped by sad and angry feelings, get stuck and unable to work through them. That someone is usually a trained counselor who may lead a peer support group of other people whose parents are divorced.

Often people of all ages think that something is wrong with them if they have to see a therapist, but a good one can teach us how to understand and express our feelings effectively. This is no different than going to a music teacher to learn to play an instrument or to a coach to learn to play a sport well. We can all benefit from working with an objective person who encourages us to explore our deeper selves. I've learned a lot about myself and grown from counseling situations, especially in groups. You and your parents can find a therapist and/or support group through your school, church, synagogue, a court mediator (see list of legal terms on page 123), or a family counseling agency suggested by the United Way.

, The skills you learn will be valuable to you in building a strong family of your own in the future. In the short run, it may seem easier to put a lid on the boiling pot of unpleasant feelings. In the long run, an explosion can result.

I'd like to hear about your reactions and discoveries as you read. Please send me your comments to include in a second edition of this book. My address is: Dr. Gayle Kimball, 445, CSU, Chico, Chico, CA 95929.

CHAPTER I

How to Survive Divorce

Jayce was five and her brother Luke was three when their parents divorced. Today they're both college students living on the west coast. They've had some rocky times, like when Jayce couldn't get along with her stepfather and moved in with her father and stepmother for a year and Luke almost didn't graduate from high school. Their father was more affectionate with Jayce, because she lived with him longer, and Luke has a hard time approaching his dad. The divorce was a tough adjustment, as "Kids are so confused, they feel like they've been torn in two." But it was even more difficult adjusting to new stepparents. What helped them survive the divorce was: "It's still vivid in my mind, my mom saying, 'This is not your fault,' 'What can I do to help you?' 'Are you OK?'"

Chris now 12, was seven when his parents separated, and his sister Rebecca was only one-year-old. He lives on the east coast and enjoys science and football (playing it and watching it, especially the Dallas Cowboys). He explains, "In the beginning I felt in the middle if I took someone's side. The other parent would feel hurt. Now when I come back from the other parent, I miss the one I left." His advice is, "Don't worry. You can't do anything about it and besides it's not your fault. Make the best of it. Hey, you can have two birthday parties. Hopefully the bad situations, like your parents' fighting, will get better. You can pray that it gets easier."

Here's a summary of the 268 experts' advice about **how to cope with divorce**, in order of frequency:

- don't blame yourself
  (overwhelmingly the most frequent suggestion),
- don't side with one parent against the other,
- talk to your parents and friends about your needs and feelings,
- remember your parents still love you,
- know things will get better,
- learn from your parents' mistakes,
- focus on your own growth, be supportive of your parents
  (They are "learning and changing just like you"),
- talk to your friends,
- don't try to get your parents back together, and
- go to a counselor.

The primary message to you from the young people surveyed for this book is that **it's not your fault** your parents divorced. But few of them say they actually felt responsible; if they blame anyone, it is one or both parents. They strongly emphasize that you should in no way blame yourself.

❋ "It's entirely your parents' problem. You had nothing to do with this. You just happen to be unlucky enough to deal with the consequences." (A ninth grader, Skylar adds that not everyone feels unlucky about a divorce.)

❋ "I felt that it was my fault and I wanted to die. Now I recognize that it wasn't my fault at all and it was probably for the better."

When kids blame themselves for their parents' divorce, they think about what they might have done wrong. In your journal writing, I'd like you to focus on what you've done right.

How to Keep a Journal

❧ You might want to buy a locked journal or write in a notebook that looks dull and unimportant to anyone who might think about reading it. Get a pen or pencil you enjoy using. Don't be concerned about your handwriting or neatness, and be sure to hide it in a safe place. Give yourself permission to write anything that pops into your mind. Don't think, just write, as our experts agree that this activity really helps to sort out feelings and thoughts. You might want to include drawings, photos, quotes, and little souvenirs you like or that remind you of something pleasant. Make your journal a place you can go to cheer yourself up as well as to dump unhappy feelings.

Journal Questions

1. List ways you've contributed to your family life.
2. What does your family like most about you? (Ask them.)
3. What five things do you most like about yourself? What are your strengths and special abilities?
4. Write out your first name, using each letter to start a word that describes you (like Jesting Excellent Designer, for my son Jed).
5. What do you think will be your strong points in your own family when you're an adult?

You can empower yourself, even in troubled times. "Please don't let television control your life; read books often and control your own life." Feeling good about yourself is a necessary tool for success and people have found ways to develop self-esteem.

How to Build Self-Esteem

Suggestions about how to build self-esteem are offered by Dr. Collette Fleuridas.

* Do positive self-talk (directions you say to yourself). Say to yourself, "I am learning to _____," "I am capable of_____," rather than "I can't_____ and "I never _____."

* Visualize (imagine the best situation). Picture yourself doing well in a situation which worries you. Fill in the sounds, smells, colors, and feelings as you picture yourself doing well on a test or telling your parent what you feel.

  Our minds are like computers that respond to programming. If you program your mind to know the right things to do and believe that you are a uniquely valuable person, you will get better results than if you program yourself negatively, as incompetent or unworthy.

* Think about difficult situations and problems as opportunities to grow and challenges to be won.

* Seek out people who value you.

* Develop your skills for assertiveness, communication, conflict resolution, and decision making, as described in this chapter.

* Observe role models you respect and find out how they manage their mistakes, doubts, and fears.

- ❧ Refuse to accept media and advertisers' definitions of looking good or popularity.

- ❧ Develop your sense of humor.

- ❧ Accept yourself as imperfect; no one else is perfect either.

- ❧ Take care of yourself; your body and mind affect each other.

This means get plenty of sleep, exercise daily, and avoid refined, fatty, salty, sugary processed foods. The more natural and fresh the food, the more food value, the more vitamins and minerals, the more energy for your body. Processed high fat foods consume energy to digest.

The second point our experts want you to know is that **things will get better:**

● "It's not the end of the world, even though it seems like it. Some very positive things are going to take place, otherwise the divorce would not be happening."

● "Have patience—in time the pain and confusion will go away."

● "Divorce is hard, but best in the long run."

● "Look at the good side. If they're not happy, how can you be happy?"

● "Change is normal though we sometimes fear its effects. You'll be happier when your parents are in a healthier relationship."

● "You may be fortunate to get a great stepparent, as I did."

Third, **take it one day and one step at a time.**

● "Take it slowly. You can't rush your emotions."

● You can't do anything about it, so "hang with it," accept it, get used to it, keep your chin up. Don't try to get your parents back together, because you can't.

● "Try not to confuse yourself by attempting to understand all the implications of the divorce at once. Things will happen quickly and you have to understand that fear and anxiety are two emotions your parents are experiencing greatly now. Try to relax, eat right, sleep plenty, and get lots of exercise. Don't do drugs to escape reality!"

● "The same problems will be there when you come down from drugs."

Fourth, the divorce does not mean your parents don't love you:

● **"Both parents still love you** even though they don't love each other."

● "They are divorcing each other, not you." (There is no legal way for a parent and child to divorce except to give up a child for adoption.)

● "Your relationship with your parents does not depend on the success of their romantic relationships."

Fifth, our experts suggest that you try to understand each parent's feelings and that you talk to both of them. They remind us about the **"power of discussion."**

○ Elaine reported, "I was afraid to tell my mom what I was thinking, so I told my friends. Now I wish I had told her."

○ "I don't express my feelings well at all, because I didn't want my mom to see me sad or upset, because she was going through a hard enough time herself."

○ "If something bothers you, tell somebody!"

○ "My parents sheltered me by not being honest. It only hurt me and taught me to keep secrets. I have always been afraid of telling the truth."

○ "If the parents make their children understand why a divorce is happening, it can be much easier!"

○ "Tell them how you feel without trying to make them feel guilty."

○ "It's OK to cry. Hold on tight because it's rough. Kids are stuck in the middle."

○ "Never be ashamed of your feelings. Someone can always understand you."

○ "Don't run away from the problem or be afraid your parents won't like what you have to say."

○ "Tell your parents, 'I love you both. Don't use me for a battling tool. Keep me out of it.'"

Ninth graders Manuel and David responded, "It's not that easy." Some parents are not yet able to be rational or fair. In that case, I suggest looking for help somewhere else. Studies of kids who succeeded despite very difficult childhoods report that they had at least one caring adult who encouraged them. This can be a grandparent, aunt or uncle, a teacher, or a friend's parent. Let an adult you trust know you would like their support and guidance.

It's also empowering to know how to express your feelings and ideas so people will listen to them. This is an area where you have control, along with how you choose to express your feelings (like pounding pillows instead of people).

If you have a major disagreement with one or both of your parents, it helps to know how to resolve conflicts. Here are techniques to solve problems effectively.

How to Resolve Conflicts

❧ Marshall Rosenberg created a formula of "compassionate communication," sometimes called **W.I.B.W.A**. This is an example of how it works. **W**hen you ask me questions about my other parent, **I feel** caught in the middle, **Because** I am loyal to both of you. **What I would like** is for you to talk directly to my other parent, **And I'm wondering** if you would not put me in the middle. Try it and see how much more effective it is than either saying nothing or blaming.

To solve a problem, ask yourself these questions and write down the answers in your journal:

Journal Questions

❀ What exactly is the problem? (For example, your parents are criticizing each other.)

❀ What are causes of the problem? (They're hurt and angry and want to let off steam or perhaps get back at the other parent.)

❀ What are possible solutions?

1. Talk to each of them individually about how torn you feel.
2. Write them letters.
3. Ask your grandparents, counselor, or clergy person to talk to them.
4. Make a sign to hold up when they start criticizing, like "Ouch! You're talking about the source of half my genes. I love you both."
5. Politely leave the room.

❀ What's the best solution?

Brainstorm other solutions, listing whatever comes to mind

without evaluation or judgment. Get more ideas from other sources, such as friends who have had the same problem, a school counselor, or books about the subject. Ask your librarian to help you in finding magazine articles and books: Many sources are listed in the bibliography at the end of this book.

Rate each possible solution on a scale of 1 to 10, with 10 being the best. Which adds up to the best solution for now? Use your intuition in making the choice about what to do. To continue our example: 1. Talk-5 points. 2. Letter-8 points. 3. Grandparents-3 points. 4. Sign-4 points. 5. Leave room-2 points. So, #2, letter, wins, indicating the first step is to write a letter suggesting specific ideas for how to improve your home life. Be sure to include what you like about your family, so your letter is read with an open mind.

How to Make a Decision

❧ A detailed way to make a decision is to make a list of your choices. Under each choice, list the pros and cons, marking a 1, 2, or 3 by each, with 3 being very important, 2 being somewhat important, and 1 being not very important. Add the totals and see which choice has the highest number.

For example, let's say you and your parents are trying to decide on your schedule back and forth between mom's house and dad's house. Let's say the choices are half time with both, most with mom, or most with dad. (A reminder that our experts insist that kids not be asked to pick one parent).

With the "half time with both" choice, the **pros** might be that:
🐾 Kids gain from having contact with both parents (3 points),

❦ You get to do different kinds of activities with each parent (2 points),

❦ You get to meet new friends at each house (1 point).

The **cons** might be that:

❧ It's hard to keep track of things (2),

❧ Your friends can't keep track of where you are (1),

❧ You have to clean up two rooms (1).

In this case, the pros win 6 to 4. Do the same for the other options and see which has the most points.

Select a date to check back to evaluate how well your solution is working. If it doesn't work, you haven't failed; you've learned more about what works and what doesn't. Like tuning up a car, it takes many adjustments, as well as ongoing maintenance, to make relationships work right.

~⸱⸱⸱⸱⸱⸱⸱~

Kids don't have a lot of power because they're dependent on their parents. Some kids feel like ping pong balls, observes counselor Tony Nethercott. Think about which problems you can help solve and which problems you have no control over. Put your energies into what you can control, like doing your best in school, and keeping away from adults' problems like arguing over child support payments. You may need to talk with a wise adult to sort out which problems you should try to solve.

One way you can **gain power** is by learning how to talk in a way that people will listen. (A good book written for parents is, *How To Talk So Your Children Will Listen and Listen So Your Children Will Talk*, by Adele Faber and Elaine Mazlish). A tool for resolving conflicts is practicing good communication skills. If you speak up without blaming, and use "I" messages, it's empowering because adults will pay attention to what you say.

How to Communicate Effectively

🐾 When you bring up a problem to work out with other people, use "I" messages. "You" message are usually attached to blame and criticism. Let's say we live together. If I say to you, "You're a slob to leave such a messy kitchen," you'll feel angry and criticize me for something in return, right? I may be telling the truth but you won't care. If I say, "I feel disorganized and out of sorts and frustrated in this kitchen and need some help," you're more likely to listen to what I have to say because you don't feel attacked and can feel empathy for my frustration.

Saying "I feel like you're a slob" is just a disguised "you" message, so watch out for "You always/never. . ." statements in any form. Stick to how you feel and you'll make more progress in solving a problem because you'll be heard. Remember that our feelings are facts and can't be argued about. If you feel some way, that's real.

Once you've defined the problem and how you feel about it, listen to the other person. "Active listening" involves repeating how the speaker feels so she or he knows you understand, even if you don't agree. This may seem like a too obvious thing to do, but most people don't listen very well. They interrupt and give advice or tell their own story. Give active listening a try with this formula, "You're feeling_____ because_____. Did I understand you correctly?"

Marc, a junior-high peer-counselor, reports that every time he uses the active listening formula people tell him to "quit messing around and get serious." It may sound insincere if you always use the formula; what matters is that you concentrate on the speaker's words, give him or her your full attention, look at the speaker, and let your friend know you understand the feelings behind his/her words, rather than switching the conversation to yourself or giving advice.

If you listen to your friends at school and not interrupt them with advice or telling about your experiences, you will find yourself appreciated because people are starving for someone to really focus on them. You can teach your best friends how to do active listening with you, too. Take turns listening to each other for half an hour and see what comes up. Giving someone your total attention allows him or her to clean out bad feelings. Then your friend can move to the next step of logically figuring out a solution. We can't be logical, though, until we have aired our anger, frustration, and grief.

～౨

The most important step to take in solving a problem is to suggest a specific solution, rather than blaming. To continue with the example of the conflict over the messy kitchen, a concrete plan is, "Let's make a chart to rotate the work of cleaning the kitchen. We each have a night a week when we cook and clean up. We post the chart so people know ahead of time." Then family members can discuss the suggestion and agree on a compromise with rewards and penalties attached to make sure it happens. People usually need to know that their action will result in clear consequences, such as doing chores results in an allowance and not doing them results in less money.

This way of dealing with conflict can be applied to problems caused by divorce—problems such as how much time to spend with each parent, or parents using kids to find out information. Here's an example. "Mom, I would like to spend more time with Dad. I love you and like to spend time with you but I miss him and need my father. I would like to have a regular schedule. How do you feel about this plan?"

Jessie asks, "What if my family won't agree to my suggestions?" Be an example for others, use "I" messages, suggest specific solutions, and do active listening. They can learn from watching you. Don't expect people to change quickly. Use what many teachers and counselors do to get the behavior they want: They reward it when it happens so that people do it again to get the reward (psychologists call this "behavior modification"). Rewards can vary from praise to food. Let's say your parent is doing better about not criticizing the other parent in front of you. Reinforce that good behavior by saying something like, "I know that you're angry at mom/dad right now, so it's hard not to be critical. I really appreciate your keeping me out of it. I'll show my thanks by doing the dishes this week without being reminded."

Sometimes you have to plant many seeds before one takes root, so don't give up. Try making your suggestion again in a different way when people are in a good mood and not too tired to listen. Sometimes being successfully assertive involves calmly repeating what you want, such as "I would like dinner time to be peaceful." People usually pay attention to consequences more than words, as parents are told in books about how to discipline children. If someone harms you emotionally or physically, you should, of course, talk to a school counselor, teacher, minister, priest, rabbi, relative, or other trustworthy adult. You deserve a healthy life.

There is **one area where you do not have to talk or listen**: Don't listen to criticism of one parent by the other parent. Their disagreements are for them to work out and not your responsibility. Nothing good can come of hearing your other parent criticized.

◗ "Speak up, don't let them tear your emotions to shreds along with theirs; it's not your fault."

◗ Don't pick a favorite parent and "don't let one parent take you away from the other."

◐ "You have the right to love both parents equally."

◐ "My mother and father tore me apart during the whole thing. When in one household that parent would constantly talk badly about the other. I was always made to feel guilty about being with one or the other. It hurts to think you are part of something that went wrong. Speak up, let them know you have some say-so and don't like being put in the middle."

◐ "I hate feeling disloyal to one parent just because I love the other one."

Do active listening and let your parent know you understand that she or he feels angry but two wrongs don't make a right. It's not right to hurt you because your parent is hurt. They're the adults and their responsibility is to protect you from harm. You don't have to listen to name-calling or yelling. Ask that it stop. You may need to leave the room if it doesn't.

Sixth, your main responsibility is to **take care of yourself.**

◉ "Focus on who you are. Spend some time alone, go on walks, find your own secret thinking place and consider your life and where you want to go, because it's up to you."

◉ "Try not to act up in school for attention. It makes things worse."

◉ "You have needs, too, so stand up for them."

◉ "Tell them what you'd like."

◉ Concentrate on "keeping your own life together."

◉ "Divorce is a tough thing to go through, especially because, as the child, you have little control of the situation occurring around you. Therapy helped me realize I don't have to carry the burdens of my parents. Taking care of myself can be difficult enough."

◉ "Don't let them make you grow up too fast. Let yourself enjoy your childhood."

● "When something goes wrong, and it doesn't have to do with you, try to let someone else handle it first."

● "Don't take on any blame for it, or you'll spend your life like I have, trying to fix everything around you. I've spent my life listening to my parents' problems. I grew up too fast. In high school I was anorexic and suicidal. I am now a recovering alcoholic. I have spent years in therapy. I spent too much time feeling sorry for myself. I have finally come to accept it and to realize that it has made me a stronger person."

~~∽~~

Young people strongly advise that you not allow yourself to be a messenger between the two parents, as "it will tear you apart." They can talk to each other on the phone, write each other notes, or use a mediator such as a counselor, minister, priest or rabbi. Let them talk to each other—not through you. Just say no, politely and firmly. It's not your job to take care of your parents or communicate for them.

You might want to write a letter to each parent. First write letters where you let out all your feelings and then tear them up so that no one sees them. Traci recommends this technique, as "it helps to get your emotions out." Then start over in a positive way by telling them what you love about them, what you appreciate that they've done for you, and how you feel about the divorce. Suggest one specific improvement, not a vague and general "be nicer," but "I'd like you to listen to me without interrupting," or "let's plan something fun at least once a week."

Psychologists agree that going through a divorce is a crisis that often lasts for about two years before things settle down. There are bound to be tense and stressful moments, so you'll need **techniques to relax** and get centered.

How to Reduce Tension

Here are quick tension reducers suggested by counselor Judith Eberhart:

🐾 Take a warm bubble bath.

🐾 Take a nap or just lie down with your eyes closed, picturing a beautiful mountain valley or beach.

🐾 Take five deep breaths from your abdominal area, rather than high up in your chest.

🐾 Drink herbal teas, such as chamomile or mint.

🐾 Stretch.

🐾 Tense and then relax each muscle, working up from feet to head.

🐾 Listen to relaxing music or a relaxation tape.

🐾 Laugh. (Read jokes, watch comedies.)

🐾 Read a favorite story you heard over and over as a child, suggests Dr. Pat Hanson.

What helps me when I'm upset or tense is to take a walk or jog, play with our dog, call a friend, write in my journal, scream while I'm riding my bike or in the shower, hit pillows, kick cardboard boxes, watch a funny video, or look at the sky and see how much bigger it is than my problem.

My students say they cope by: listening to music, taking a bubble bath with music and candles, watching the comedy station on television, taking naps, going on walks, talking to friends, crying, making a list of all they have to do and doing the most important things first—then giving themselves rewards, and taking short trips. Take good care of yourself during this stressful time. You can learn a lot and become a stronger person.

Journal Questions

1. What is one improvement you'd like to see in your family?
2. What specific suggestion do you have for improvement?
3. Try using the **W.I.B.W.A.** model of asking for change. How did it work?
4. What is the most relaxing tension reducer for you?
5. What did you do this week that most deserves applause?
6. What was the most unusual thing that happened this week?
7. What are you looking forward to next weekend?
8. If you could give yourself a new first name, what would it be?
9. Whom do you most admire?

CHAPTER 2

MAKING SENSE OF THE SEPARATION

Jayce and Luke's parents married when her dad was in medical school and her mom was only 19 years old. They came from the same religious background, and she liked his parents. When Jayce was eight she asked about the divorce and her dad told her information she wasn't ready to hear: "I don't want to know about that side of him. I don't think I should have to judge my father and wish he hadn't told me," she said. The effect of the divorce on her is, "It's a very maturing experience. I felt like I needed to take care of my brother."

Chris "could see it coming. I can remember them fighting as far back as when I was four or five. They are two different people, who argued about the simplest things. Whenever a decision had to be made, they would totally disagree. It really wasn't a surprise. No one really told me." A couple of times he wondered, "What did I do?" but his dad frequently told him not to blame himself.

What's hard for him now is his sister is "better than me in Mom's eyes. At least over at my dad's I am equal to her," and he misses one parent when he's at the other parent's home. The divorce has given him more time to get to know and love his dad; because of his parents' frequent fighting, he used to think of his dad as the "bad guy." He's also learned to stay away from fights himself.

As in Chris' family, some parents didn't clearly **explain why they are separating**; they just say that dad is moving out or going

away. Parents who do a good job of explaining usually say they couldn't get along and weren't in love anymore. They tell their kids that they in no way caused the divorce and that they will continue to see both their parents.

Although most kids are upset, sad, angry, confused, or scared when they find out about their parents' separation, time brings a different viewpoint. One of our experts pointed out that it helps to know that there are **stages of dealing with grief.** This idea is the basis of some support groups for kids going through their parents' divorces. Most of us experience these stages at various times in our lives, as when a pet dies or a friend moves away. Group leader Brian Holderman says we even go through it in a mini-version when the alarm rings in the morning. We feel angry about being woken up and we stay in denial by hitting the snooze button, until we move to acceptance and look forward to the day about to unfold.

The idea stems from physician Elisabeth Kübler-Ross who identified the stages of grieving the loss of a relationship as:

- denial (They'll get back together.)
- anger (They should have tried harder.)
- bargaining (If I get the grades they want me to get in school, maybe Dad/Mom will come back home.)
- depression (I'm always going to be sad and tired.)
- acceptance (It's for the best.)
- Hope is a last stage, added by "Stages," an Irvine, California, school program for students going through major changes.

Journal Questions

1. Which of the six stages are you in now?

2. What stages have you passed through?

3. Where do you see yourself headed?

4. Have you experienced denial?

5. Can you think of other times you experienced a major change in your life that you didn't like and the emotional stages that followed?

People can bounce back and forth between stages; feelings are never as neat and tidy as a list suggests. Lynne Reyman, a counselor, reports that the ups and downs sometimes feel like a roller coaster ride, but this is normal and won't last forever. Jennifer advises, "The feelings will always be there, but you will learn how to deal with them when they come up. Don't be ashamed to talk about your feelings even years after the divorce."

Therapist Ro Bolen, after much experience with groups for children of divorce, observes that, "Most children don't come to the stage of acceptance until late teens or early twenties." Another counselor, Ann Marie Simmons, who works in a school-based program, points out that parents and kids may work through the stages of grieving differently. Carrie saw her parents go through "stages of anger, fear, regret, remorse, denial, hatred, and more. Don't let it affect you too much, as there are brighter days ahead," Carrie advises.

Many parents put their kids on hold during the crisis period, reports school social worker Liz McGonagle, so the kids don't get the support they need to grieve. They stay "in denial," acting as if the divorce didn't happen, so it takes them longer to get to the acceptance stage. When the parents are feeling good enough to start dating, their kids may not be at all ready and find shifting of attention to the new adults very disturbing, says Ms. Simmons.

The majority of our experts did get to the last stage of acceptance.

They grew to believe that the divorce was for the best after realizing that their parents couldn't live together happily. They say the main reason their parents couldn't get along was they were too different. Some parents got married too young and grew apart, had different values and interests, didn't communicate well, or one parent had an alcohol or drug problem. Some parents found a new love while they were still married which, needless to say, was not popular with anyone else in the family.

~

More **blamed their father** than their mother for the divorce, explaining that he cheated on his wife, was a jackass, a workaholic or an alcoholic, etc. This may be because kids are more likely to live with their mothers, hear their views, be dependent on them, and feel protective. Since dads usually are expected to leave the family home when parents separate, it may seem to kids that their father is leaving them, and this causes hurt and anger. But it's not fair to blame dads for leaving just because that's what men are supposed to do.

I wondered if the sex of the child makes a difference in their view of the cause of the divorce. It does. More boys give neutral explanations, such as their parents married too young, while girls are about evenly divided between those who give neutral reasons and those who blame their father.

Only a small percent of both sexes blame their mother, even though it usually takes two to tango. We may need to do a better job of preparing boys to be husbands and fathers, as well as to be successful breadwinners. It's hard to live up to the male role of breadwinning, performance, and competition. Most of our experts urge you to listen to both parents and not take sides, unless one parent is abusive or an addict. Counselor Judy Osborne reports that, "I like to help kids understand that it's never too late to ask the questions and to expect to have to understand the divorce over and over again."

Journal Questions

1. List the reasons why your parents separated.
2. Why do you think they got married? If you are not clear about the reasons for their marriage and divorce and the changes that happened between these two events, ask them when you're ready. Ask like a reporter not a blamer.
3. What can we do instead of blaming someone?

It's important to understand your parents' relationship because **people tend to repeat the familiar**. That is, we tend to pick someone to date and then marry who is like our parent of the other gender; we pick what feels natural, what we're used to. Sometimes we pick someone the opposite of this parent, but that still means we are deciding on the basis of unfinished business.

The better you understand what kept your parents' marriage from lasting, the more wisely you will select your own life partner. If they married too young, you can decide to wait. If she married him because he was like a sturdy oak to depend on, and if he married her because she was lively and emotionally expressive, and then they got bored or out of touch because they didn't have enough in common, you can decide *not* to pick someone because he or she expresses a quality you lack. If they spent too little time developing their couple relationship, you can plan to schedule a date each weekend with your future spouse and regular time to check in with each other about your feelings.

People whose parents divorced when they were very young don't remember **how their life changed**. The most frequent reply from the experts is that they became more responsible, mature, and independent than others their age. Studies confirm this as a pattern for children of divorce. Kids say they became more responsible as they did more work about the house and helped care for their younger sister or brother: "You are forced to grow up very rapidly." Positive effects occurred more often than negative ones. Those whose parents yelled and argued are glad for the peace and quiet that followed the separation. As one of the experts reminds us, "There are a lot of successful people who grew up in single–parent homes."

Some kids enjoy their parents more after the conflict has ended and they have quality time with each one. Some report that their mothers became more independent, finished school, and got better jobs. Some people say their parents became happier, especially in a healthy second marriage. And the young people gain from "twice as much love as someone who only has two parents. I have two whole and unique families, with twice the support, and many different role models." Children learn about relationships and value "how important a family is." The upside of the family shake-up is, "I realize marriage is fragile and requires work to keep things together."

Can you imagine thinking that your parents' **divorce is for the best**? The majority of our experts report that:

🦋 "The divorce worked out for the best because my parents are happier not being married."

🦋 "We didn't lose the feeling of family."

🦋 "I enjoy my parents apart. I'm able to know each separately. They should have divorced earlier."

🦋 "It's better now that they're not fighting. I guess they do it away from us."

🦋 "We have a bigger stepfamily."

Don, 18, who read a draft of this book, wants me to tell you that more in-depth mention is needed of the fact that divorce can be positive. In his family, his father was emotionally abusive to everyone and hit the boys. When the two brothers found out that he was sexually abusing their sister, they went to their mother and said their father had to go. She agreed and he left the next day. "The financial disadvantage of separation is nothing compared to the emotional gain for all family members. Nobody wins, but a continuous suffering is stopped, and recovery can begin. From the age of 11, I knew that me and my family would benefit from the separation." When it took place, Don was 15, and he felt relief, not loss.

For some of our young people, the **effects of the divorce are still painful**. "There's no more home sweet home and much less delicious home-cooked meals." Some kids are home alone more because their mothers are working longer hours or going out on dates. "I have to do things my mom would normally do." "My family was just destroyed. Mom took two jobs, and Dad left. For a long time we really had no parents. I am angry that they split and threw our family away." Some report feeling lonely. Some people got poorer when one household became two and they moved into a smaller home. Some report that the relationship with their noncustodial parent suffered and they miss having two parents to help them grow up.

Some became insecure and less trusting. A boy says, "female relationships are harder to develop. I'm careful about my relationships." Another says, "I'm more cautious; I look harder at girls now." One girl reports, "I still feel I am not settled and nothing will last forever. It seems like everything could disappear tomorrow. It's a feeling of constant uncertainty. I feel like I'm always looking for something but I can never find it."

Counselor Judy Osborne reports that an eating disorder clinic in Boston found all of the young women they served had experienced their parents' divorce as preteen girls! Eating disorders are sometimes an attempt to be in control when other parts of one's life are not going the way one would like. Professor Neil Kalter found that the effects of a divorce do stay with young people and they may need special support during the various stages of growing up. You need to let your parents know what would help you most to develop your potential.

A minority of our young people still have mainly unhappy feelings years after the divorce:

- "I wish my parents still lived together."
- "I miss the family atmosphere."
- "It's hard when Mom says we are still a family because it doesn't feel like a family anymore."
- "I feel lost and I want to have a whole family."
- "It's like the one stable thing you always counted on and trusted in is no longer there."
- "It changed everyone's lifestyle."
- "It's been hard ever since. Money was tight and babysitters were too common and mom worked a lot."
- "I miss my dad."
- "I don't like going back and forth between two homes."
- "I still resent my mom for leaving the marriage."
- "I still think they broke up because of me."
- "They tore my life apart with manipulation and games."
- "It still kills me. I still believe they could get along well."
- "I felt deserted and disappointed in my parents and adults in general."
- "I have more responsibilities now."

  ※ Do you share any of these feelings from the positive or negative lists?

You hear a lot about how kids of divorce have more problems. Researchers Constance Ahrons and Joan Kelly point out though that **problems make news**. Researchers agree that the majority of children experiencing a divorce go though a crisis period for a few years following the divorce, especially boys, but most get on track again. It's not the divorce that is the long-term problem, it's feeling caught in continued conflict between parents and the loss of effective parenting that hurts kids. This is often true for single moms who have trouble disciplining their boys.

Children of divorce are slightly more likely to have emotional and school problems than children with two happily married parents. However, Dr. E. Mavis Hetherington points out that kids do better in a well-functioning single-parent family than with married parents who are fighting. Like other experts, she found that kids do best when parents are warm, firm, listen to their children, and maintain a secure routine, rather than when parents are either authoritarian or permissive.

Professor Frank Mott followed 1,700 children of divorce for almost ten years. He found that the most important influence on how well teenagers are doing is the level of the teens' conflict with their mothers. If the conflict level is high, these kids have lower grades and more emotional problems than kids with less conflict. He also found that Caucasian boys (but not boys of other ethnic backgrounds) who do not have contact with their fathers have more emotional problems than other groups of kids.

Dr. Mott's study means that you should put effort into reducing conflict with your mother, if it exists. This may require the help of an unprejudiced third person like a counselor or clergy person who can help you practice techniques to solve conflicts and really listen to each other's feelings. It also means that you should let your parents know how important your father is to you.

Therapists who lead support groups for children of divorce, told me their are common problems they hear from kids. The **common problems** the 20 counselor report are:

♥ Kids taking their anger out on other kids, by getting in fights at school, or turning it inward and getting depressed or sick,

♥ Kids feeling pulled between their two parents as when they use children as messengers ("Tell your father he owes $80 in child support.") and fight with each other,

♥ Worrying if they caused the divorce,

♥ Wanting their parents to get back together,

♥ Not getting enough attention when parents are upset by the crisis of divorce or abuse of alcohol and drugs, plus having the parent unload their bad feelings on the child,

♥ Feeling angry about the lack of child support payments and having to move to a smaller home,

♥ Grieving over a parent who drops out,

♥ Not being able to understand their feelings so they come out in stomachaches and headaches,

♥ Not feeling free to express their feelings to their parents,

♥ Getting attached to a parent's girlfriend or boyfriend only to have them breakup,

♥ Adjusting to a new stepparents, stepbrothers, and stepsisters (especially an issue for girls and their stepmothers),

♥ Dealing with a second divorce, and

♥ Worrying about their own future ability to avoid a divorce.

A school counselor in Michigan reports that lately they have heard more about difficulties between brothers and sisters, and their stepsiblings, sometimes bordering on violence.

Our youth agree that divorce is painful but report that if the child has continuing support and love from caring adults he or she does fine. Julie's is the ideal situation: "I don't believe the divorce phased me that much. I don't remember a time that my father wasn't there when I wanted him to be." On the other side, Kara's situation is exactly what must be avoided. After her parents divorced, when she was 13:

> *They were so absorbed in their own lives they forgot about me (not on purpose.) I was lonely for either of them. I went from being confident and happy to depressed and unstable. I began to get healthy again when I came to college. I had to do it on my own (except financially). I feel like my parents missed out on my life from ages 13 to 18. I was crying out for help and attention. If I want something now I get it myself.*

The large **majority of our experts are doing well**, as indicated by the fact that most report they are "B" or "A" students. When asked to list three personal qualities they were proud of, most did so. Very few listed only one or two qualities. It's the kids who felt they had to take care of a parent emotionally, or who felt abandoned by one or both parents, who are still hurting.

Dr. Constance Ahrons reports, "It's not the divorce so much as the way parents handle it." She estimates that about half the parents are able to reduce conflict, keep a routine so that kids feel secure, and work together to parent well. Kids with these kinds of effective parents have few differences in outcome from kids with married parents.

Do any of these situations apply to you? Is there anything that you can suggest to your parents to correct a problem caused by the divorce? Nicole responds that, "Parents aren't always going to be receptive to advice from their kids. They are emotionally struggling, too. There is a right time and a wrong one to bring up the subject."

Brent adds, "Make sure you aren't sending a message to the kid that it's their responsibility to hold up the family. This could lead to further guilt." Joan, the mother of a daughter who was sexually abused by her father agrees, "Oftentimes, especially in drug/alcohol/abuse situations, children are forced to behave as adults and switch roles to become the nurturer rather than the child." Your job is to do well in school, develop your talents, establish friendships, define your values and beliefs, and appreciate your uniqueness, not to be a parent.

Journal Questions

1. How has life changed for you since the divorce?
2. How have you changed as a person?
3. What are the most important things you've learned because of the divorce?
4. Have you experienced any of the common problems named by the counselors?
5. What do you do to solve a problem?
6. Whom do you depend on for support and understanding?
7. If you were going to become a cartoon or comic character, whom would you pick?
8. How would your life be different if you woke up tomorrow as the other gender? Would you choose to stay that way?

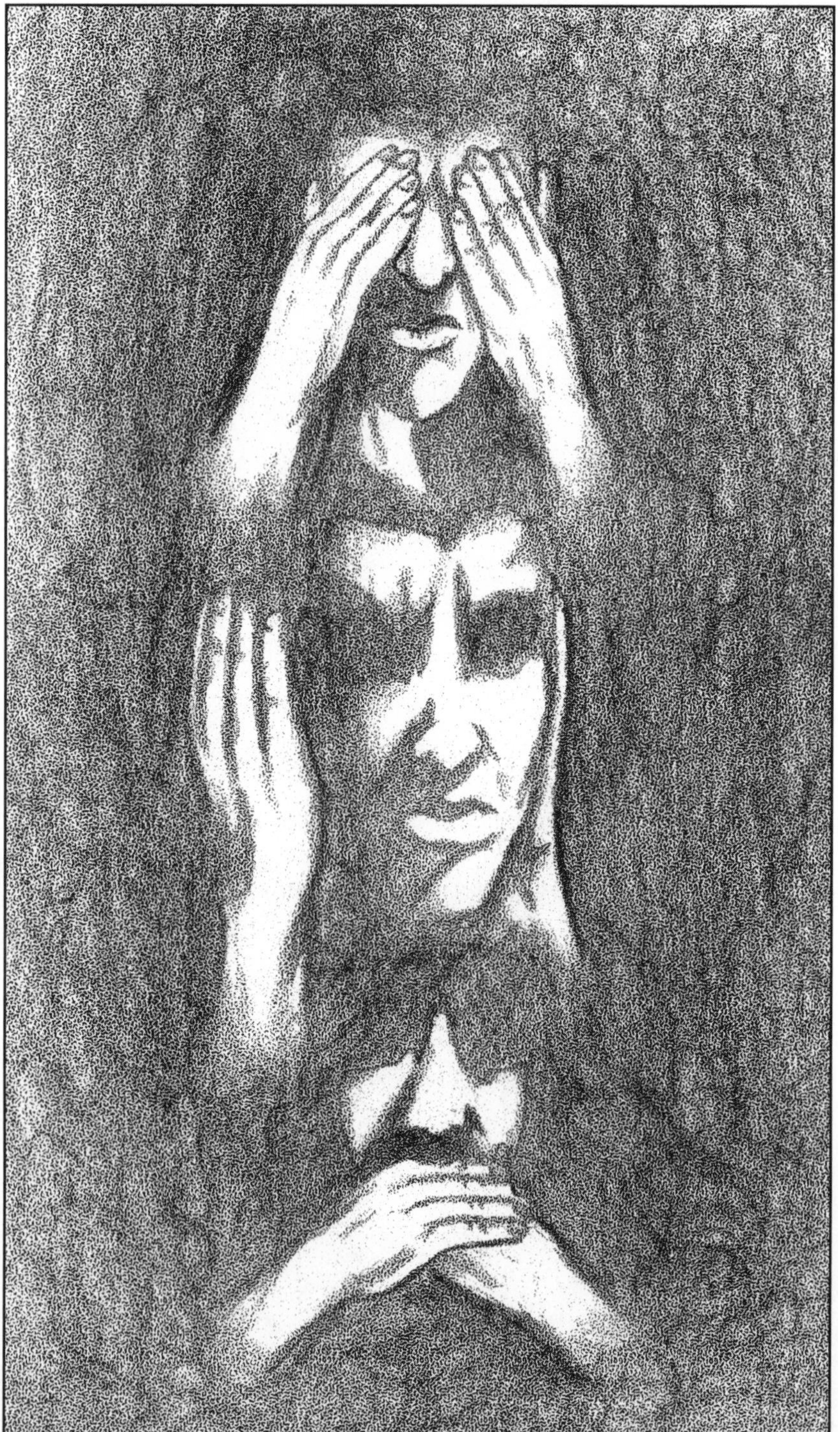

DRAWING BY ANTHONY MORANO

CHAPTER 3

NAMING YOUR FEELINGS

Jayce is open with her feelings, like her mother. Her brother Luke is quiet about them, like his father, and he doesn't like to open up to his mom, who is his main parent. He's had a harder time than Jayce doing well in school and finding himself. The first time he really opened up to his sister was as a high school senior, when he told her he felt he had disappointed his dad and himself with his school grades.

Chris was protective of his parents during the separation: "I really didn't talk too much to other people. I thought my problems shouldn't be theirs. I just did things to keep my mind off the situation." His mom doesn't like to talk with him about the divorce either and changes the subject when it comes up, but his stepmother encourages him to talk with her and his dad. He used to think that having a talk meant he'd done something wrong, but "now it's starting to mean something good. I usually don't like to talk, but when I do, it makes me feel better."

He's changing about talking with friends, too: "I used to think why would people want to hear about my problems, they'd think I was weird. Now, with more people having divorces, there are kids at school that I talk to about our parents being divorced. About half my friends' parents are divorced."

Simply **saying how you feel** is the first step in surviving divorce (or any other emotional challenge). Brian Holderman is a teacher who leads divorce support groups through his church. He reports that many of his elementary school students, "have trouble pinpointing the feelings so they become numb. Stored anger and depression can form into stomachaches and headaches." He emphasizes the importance of writing in a journal and seeing a counselor to learn the language of expressing feelings. ▓ Do you think Luke and Chris might be numbing their feelings of sadness and anger? Do you think boys have less encouragement to reveal their feelings because they are supposed to be tough Marlboro men?

Mr. Holderman teaches his students that there are different degrees of feelings, such as irritation/anger/rage: These are different intensities of feeling mad. Sometimes it takes a while to figure out that feeling so tired you just want to lie on your bed and look at the ceiling is depression, a kind of sadness. He also finds that boys are more likely to outwardly express their anger than girls, so being male or female also has an impact on how we get our feelings out.

School counselor Tony Nethercott agrees that his students often don't know how they're feeling or realize they're blaming themselves for the divorce. He teaches them that its OK to have all kinds of feelings, as long as you don't take them out on your little brother or sister or hurt people. Kids he sees range from being in denial to wanting to kill the world. Some start fighting in school without realizing why.

Some of his elementary school students are helped by taking out their anger on a four-foot purple lion in his office; they throw it, beat it, jump on it. They may do this with a puppet who represents a brother or sister, for example. He finds that some young people can write things in their journal they can't say out loud, a very helpful tool for expressing feelings. Giving caring attention to his students works wonders, even if it's just playing a game together.

Don didn't have someone like Mr. Nethercott to help him sort out his feelings. When he was 15, his parents divorced. Instead of

ing through his anger, he distracted himself by breaking the law. He
tells us:

> *I wouldn't accept any help. Me and my sister went to a coun-*
> *selor a couple of times, but we didn't want anybody else pok-*
> *ing around in our business. I wasn't ready to share. I'm real*
> *stubborn. I didn't want anybody to know my weaknesses. I*
> *took a lot of my frustrations out by stealing. I got a rush off of*
> *it and it helped me forget my regular life.*
>
> *But it didn't help. I quit when I was 17 because I learned*
> *some lessons the hard way. I talked to some wise people, to*
> *counselors. I realized I felt bad about myself, I had low self-*
> *esteem. Counseling only works if you're ready for it. I can be*
> *so stubborn. I decided to focus on school and work, to start*
> *obeying the law, and put my powers into other things.*

Journal Questions

1. What do you do when you are feeling angry? Sad? Depressed? Afraid?
2. Whom do you tell about your feelings?
3. Have you put souvenirs of happy memories in your journal yet?
4. What happens if you don't express your deep feelings?
5. How do you think you would express anger and sadness
   if you were the other sex?

Here's **how young people feel when their parents separate**
(listed in the order of the most common feelings), with examples
of their comments. Some people were too young to remember the
divorce, but the large majority of our experts have negative feel-

ings about the divorce.

♢ Upset, hurt, shocked, crushed, devastated, stunned. "I felt my heart was physically breaking." "It hurt because I needed both of them to be there for me."

♢ Sad. "I cried forever."

♢ Angry and deserted. "I felt they were doing this to me." "I was afraid I wouldn't see my dad again." "I spent the next 10 years worrying that I would lose my mom, but now it seems normal."

♢ Glad because it stopped their fighting (or being around a parent addicted to alcohol or drugs). "It's better because I can speak my mind without getting thrown across the room or backhanded by my drunk father."

♢ Surprised and confused. "I never saw them argue. I thought everything was fine." "I did not understand for a couple of years, so of course I wanted them back together."

♢ Guilty. "I thought I was bad and that my dad didn't want to spend time with us any more." "I used to think it was something I did."

▓ Which of these feelings do you share? Figuring this out can be easier said than done. Some young people didn't let themselves feel because it's unpleasant, they didn't know how, or they didn't feel their parents could handle it. These are typical comments:

● "I kept my emotions inside by not talking about it."

● "I repressed my feelings for a year, like a calm before a big storm, but you know something major is going to happen and life will never be the same."

● "I thought it didn't affect me, but I found out it did."

● "I blocked out memories of parts of my life from five to twelve."

● "If you don't talk about it, you won't be able to deal with it and might live in a fantasy world for a while (like I think I did)."

● "Instead of talking about my feelings, I got stomachaches."

● "I got into fights at school a lot. Now I think it was my anger about the divorce."

● "Tell kids they should talk to someone. I didn't want to sound like I was whining, but now I know it's brave to say what you feel and it gets rid of the idea you could have stopped the divorce."

Don't be like an ostrich that sticks its head in the sand to avoid danger, as you leave your rear exposed. Unconscious feelings can run your life in a way you may not like. The solution is to face them, let yourself feel them, and allow the healing process to start. If you don't, you'll attract people to repeat the pattern you're familiar with and haven't completed. This may not be enjoyable. Counselor Steve Flowers points out that if you carry a skunk around long enough, you end up smelling like one.

For example, a person with an alcoholic parent may learn a certain pattern of behavior and repeat it by being attracted to alcoholic partners until he learns a healthier way of relating. Or someone who stuffs her anger may be attracted to people who act out their anger in dramatic ways. Similarly, people watch soap operas or sports to try and fulfill their longing for romance or victory, instead of creating romance or adventure in their own lives. Just because we ignore our feelings doesn't mean they don't have a powerful effect, like a car whose driver is asleep at the wheel isn't aware the car is moving until a crash occurs.

A 23-year-old whose parents divorced when she was two years old explains:

Although I was so young, I know it affected me in countless ways. My mom tells me about when I was four and we passed a church wedding. I asked a million questions and then woke up crying in the middle of the night. It happened again when I was nine and found their wedding album in the attic. But both my parents are way better matched with their current spouses.

It may not be easy to identify feelings, buried deep in the unconscious mind. Like an iceberg, the biggest part isn't visible to your conscious mind. The unconscious is not just a passive storehouse for memories, but an active one. It doesn't use the language of words, but of symbols, stories, and pictures. It works through feelings, solving problems. The most direct link from the unconscious to the conscious mind is dreams. You dream every night and can probably learn to remember them if you feel it is important.

To give you an example of **how the unconscious mind works**, I had a series of dreams, over several months, in which I was asked to teach math, a nightmare for me. In different dreams I struggled with teaching math. Finally, at the end of the series of dreams many months later, I said NO. The principal accepted my decision. My unconscious mind was practicing being assertive. The conscious mind would have used logic, saying, "I need to learn to say no to unreasonable requests," but my unconscious mind practiced in a drama to arrive at the same conclusion.

✳ If you remember any **dreams**, write them in your journal. It saves much time in therapy if you discuss your dreams with your counselor, parents, or friend. They probably won't make any sense at first, but they will after you discover patterns and learn the meaning of the stories your unconscious mind uses.

How to Remember Your Dreams

🐾 When you go to bed at night, tell yourself you would

like to remember your dreams. Put your journal by your bed. When you wake up in the morning, ask yourself what you dreamed. Don't get out of bed, or your dreams will roll back into your unconscious mind. Make your mind blank, like a TV screen, and watch what comes up. Sometimes you will be able to remember two or three dreams. These messengers from the hidden part of your mind are pearls to treasure even if they're unpleasant.

After a month or so, read your dream journal and see what repeats. The most common dreams are about anxiety, so be prepared to see these. Examples are being chased, or put in jail, or arriving at a test after everyone has left. For me, it's going skiing and forgetting my skis or teaching and forgetting my notes. Other common dreams are about wishes, like dreaming about food when you're hungry. What are the most vivid dreams you remember?

Another good way to see what you feel is to **create movie-like scenes** with little objects on sand or soil. Some therapists have these sand trays in their offices or you could make your own simply by arranging miniature toys and natural objects like stones. Don't think much; just arrange things. See what drama you make up and what this reflects about your present family relationships.

We usually need a therapist to help figure out what we've created because it's hard to see something we're close to. (A therapist who read this wants me to add that sand tray is a form of therapy that requires training, it's not just something to pick up and do. Brent, 18, thinks that friends and other trusted people can often help, too.) This activity is usually designed for young children, but any age can learn from it, as most adults don't know a lot about their unconscious mind.

I've enjoyed doing this with a friend at the beach and comparing what we've built.

Drawing and painting are other ways to encourage your unconscious mind to let you know what's going on in there. Please stop reading now and draw your family members. Don't judge your abilities as an artist; ask your deeper self to speak for you. " If you think, then your true feelings may not come out." Think about whom you draw rather than how you draw. Use crayons, colored pencils, or paint, so you can include the feelings represented by colors. Red, for example, might indicate anger, and gray might indicate sadness. Include yourself in the drawing. Write in your journal what clues your drawings give you about how you are feeling now.

Journal Questions

1. How do you feel about the connections between the people in your art?
2. Who's big? Who's little?
3. Who's close? Who's far apart?
4. Who is nearer to whom?
5. Who is up and who is down?
6. What kinds of expressions do they have on their faces?
7. Where are they looking?
8. What are they doing?
9. Who is missing, or in profile, or is drawn with missing body parts?
10. Are the colors dark or bright?

It's interesting to have other people your age do the same drawing exercise and share with each other. In a support group for young people whose parents are divorcing, this exercise is very helpful. Your personal counselor, a school counselor, a clergy person, or a youth agency like a YWCA or YMCA might be able to find this kind of group for you, as described in the next chapter.

Journal Questions

1. How have your feelings changed since you first learned about your parents' separation?
2. What do your dreams, drawings, and fantasies tell you about what your unconscious mind is working on now?
3. What was the most fun thing you did this year?
4. What country would you most like to visit?
5. What's the most fun trip you've ever taken?

CHAPTER 4

GETTING HELP

Jayce's counselor "wanted me to talk about my feelings. We used dolls and did role-playing. She was a very kind, supportive person, always listening to the things I had to say. We didn't always talk about the divorce; we talked about my daily life—school and friends. She tried to help me keep a positive attitude, always affirming that it wasn't my fault."

Chris coped by keeping busy to "keep my mind off the situation." (This, of course, doesn't allow healing to occur.) He, his sister, and his mother went to a counselor during the separation, but "it didn't have an effect because we went for a short time. He told me it takes two people to make a divorce and tried to interpret what happened." Chris' mom is going to see a counselor again and Chris is thinking about seeing her, too, because she is not just a "basic counselor," like the ones at his school, but specializes in divorce. Another source of support is his younger sister, as "me and Rebecca are a team, we go back and forth together. It's easier to do it with someone else."

༄

Dr. Judith Wallerstein is studying 60 families many years after the divorce; she reports that few of the children had help in coping with the divorce. Our experts advise you to **reach out** to others for support during the divorce crisis.

✴ "Look for real friends, those who can listen without being critical."

✳ "Talk about it with kids who've already experienced it."

✳ Go to a counselor; it's "not so strange."

✳ "Find a role model, an adult who can teach good skills and help build your self-esteem."

✳ "Divorce is a hard thing. It doesn't have to run your life but it is always there. One just has to take life day by day. It's a great idea to have an understanding adult who isn't the parent to befriend a child going through divorce."

✳ "Spend time with other relatives to help retain the feeling of family."

Our experts report that their **friends** are the most frequent source of support during the separation and divorce, followed by parents, other relatives, and siblings. Good friends understand that it is OK to cry, especially when they have gone through the same experience. "Friends became my family," Walt reported.

Schools can build on this natural source of peer support and provide **groups for kids** whose parents are divorcing. The schools in Irvine, California provide "Stages" groups led by counselors for students who are coping with "life changes" including divorce, death, and moving. Students are pulled out of class, as are students in Holland, Michigan's intermediate school support program. Some New York schools have a "Banana Splits" support group for students who volunteer to join; this program has expanded to states like Hawaii and Virginia.

These groups let students realize other people are going through the same problems and share coping techniques. One of my older divorced students successfully proposed the idea to her son's elementary school principal, showing that when you speak up to suggest a program, you can really make a difference. (Resources are listed on page 137.)

A family law judge suggested the formation of Kids' Turn in the San Francisco Bay Area. Young people meet in one group and parents in another, using a curriculum developed for the groups. Kids in the 10 to 14 age group engage in learning activities like writing group stories, creating pictures, and writing a newsletter for their parents. The kids role-play to practice communication skills. The groups are not seen as therapy but educational.

For our experts, **parents** come in second place as a source of support, followed closely by **relatives** such as grandparents, aunts, and uncles, probably because some parents are so upset they cannot give much peace of mind to their children. Brothers and sisters were fourth. When kids go back and forth between two households, siblings provide secure companionship.

Shelly explains, "Having my brother with me as I moved back and forth every week was great. He was the one constant in my life, even if I didn't like him at the time." An only child says, "If you have brothers and sisters, count your blessings. All I ever wanted was a sibling to share my experience with so I wouldn't be so alone." Pets are helpful to some: "I talk to my pets; I know it's weird but they give me needed unconditional love."

More young people mention depending on themselves, without support from others, than mention going to counselors. Although counselors are lower on the list of helpful people, if you can find a way to get to a counselor or support group, please go, as "our counselor helped a lot. We all went." They see many divorces and know what causes them, how to cope with them, and how to teach communication skills. And as an outsider, he or she should be able to see clearly and without bias or prejudice. Tony Nethercott is a school counselor. When his son asked him if he was a good counselor to his own children, he said "No," because he is their father and too emotionally involved.

It's useful to talk with other people who have used the services of a counselor for their recommendations. Some parents have insurance that will pay for counselors and some schools, agencies, and religious groups have them for free, because many families can't afford to pay a counselor. They're usually expensive, like using the services of most professionals.

Although I think **counselors** are usually needed to get through a divorce, to be a fair reporter, I have to say that some of the ninth grade students who read this book are critical of their counselors, as were some of the college students.

● "They don't work for everybody: I think you should make a point of that."

● "I hate shrinks."

● "A counselor makes you feel like you can't do things for yourself." "Counselors don't work as well as everybody thinks."

● "I tried it once and it didn't do a thing for me. The best thing for me was time, time helps it all."

● "To seek help it doesn't have to be a shrink."

Jed explained that counselors are adult authority-figures, other adults who are bossing you around. "If you say anything back they get irritated. You don't feel close to them, or trust them, so you're not going to tell them your deepest secrets. It helps to have someone to listen to you, so talk to a relative or friend you trust." This distrust is not unique to young people. Yvonne reports, "My parents went to a counselor but my dad wasn't open to the idea of letting someone know how he feels. It really hurt the relationship. Part of it was his pride and part was that he didn't really care to repair the relationship." If you feel mistrustful and dominated by your counselor, explain this and let him or her know when you feel "power tripped." This could open up useful emotional material to work through. Sometimes people dump their anger on their counselor because it seems safe, as therapist Anne Giel observes.

How to Make Counseling Work

🐾 Be patient and don't expect instant results. You need to be willing to open up to a counselor rather than try to fool her or him or turn it into a game to see how little you can tell. Take charge by telling the counselor what you want to work on. If you don't know how you're really feeling, suggest drawing or sand trays or bring in your dream journal to get started. Talk about what you like and don't like about yourself, what you want to build on and how you want to grow, or whatever is important to you. Ideally you can find a young peoples' group where the kids have power in their numbers.

Other sources of strength mentioned by the young people are teachers, religion, engaging in activities like sports, and pets. Deborah Chad, a student intern at the Children's Rights Council, recommends their book list and phone line (1-800-787-Kids). A newsletter is available for kids of divorce, called *Kids Express*, designed for elementary school kids. (Addresses are on page 139.) 🌼 Make a list of your sources of strength and support.

Meditation or prayer is centering, calming, grounding, and a source of answers. If you go to church, temple, or mosque, you might want to ask your clergy person for ideas about how to pray. Meditation involves putting aside a quiet time each day. The point is to quiet the mind that hops around like a monkey, in order to get to our deeper source of truth and strength.

How to Relax

❧ Different techniques are used to quiet the mind, so you can relax and tune in to your deeper self. Count your breath (one, inhale; two, exhale; one, inhale. . .), listen to a meditation tape, look at a beautiful photograph, and repeat a phrase such as "serenity and love." By concentrating on your breathing or a phrase and coming back to it as thoughts pop up, you will calm the mind. This daily quiet period is good for the body too and helps you stay healthy in stressful times. Throughout the day, it can help to repeat something positive like "I am calm, relaxed, and centered."

Take deep breaths and visualize the most peaceful place you can possibly imagine. My friend Gordon sets his watch to beep every hour, which reminds him to take a deep relaxing breath. I like it when he's around because I can take time to get calm too.

These last two chapters may give you new techniques to experiment with to find out how useful they are for you. You have plenty of time, so start with one new technique that seems most workable now, and come back to the others when you have practiced the first one. Don't expect to become a polished communicator, decision maker, and relaxed conflict resolver in a flash. It's a lifetime process of growth. I've been working on these skills for years and have infinitely more to learn. Growth is what makes life interesting, not perfection.

Journal Questions

1. Who helps you to feel cared about and understood?
2. Have you shared experiences with other young people whose parents divorced?
3. What helps you to feel calm and peaceful?

DRAWING BY NADIA PURI

CHAPTER 5

FAMILY FUN TO GET YOU THROUGH HARD TIMES

Jayce and her mom's family like to ski and go to the ocean together. Luke and his stepfather like to hunt and work on cars. At Chris' mom's house, he goes shopping with his mom, and they see a movie sometimes. That's the only thing the three of them do together, he says. At his dad's house, they play video games, play basketball and football in the back yard, and go for walks in a nearby park.

Because **good times are the glue that holds relationships together**, it's helpful to establish a regular schedule of family fun time. For a different book project, my students and I asked over 200 employed parents what their families did for fun. In order of frequency, they said: sports, travel, watch videos or movies, cook and eat together, play games, go shopping, talk with family and friends, visit friends, and go to church or church-related activities. How would your family answer this question?

Dr. Barbara Polland suggests these ideas for family fun:

🦋 Twice a year a parent wakes up a kid in the middle of the night for a surprise snack and chat.

🦋 Camp outside on a warm night.

🦋 Give free gifts to each other on holidays—like a back rub or help with cleaning a room.

🦋 Make a family collage, an artwork with photographs, souvenirs, and drawings.

🦋 Have a backward meal with dessert first or have a "favorite friend" dinner where each person invites a buddy.

🦋 Make dinner special by turning off the television and discussing topics like what funny things happened this week or, if you could remove one person from your life last week, who would it be? (Dave suggests not including family members in this last exercise, because it caused lots of arguments in his family.)

(Dr. Polland would like your additions: Sent them to Equality Press.)

I've collected other ideas for fun. Although some teens commented that some of these activities are for youngsters, I think we all have a young kid inside us who enjoys being invited to play. I do. . .

🛋 Put on rock 'n roll music and dance in your living room.

🛋 Paint a family mural on a big piece of butcher paper (sometimes you can get ends of paper rolls free from newspaper publishers).

🛋 Finger paint or toe paint.

🛋 Make chalk drawings on the sidewalk near your home.

🛋 Make crafts together—get ideas from craft stores, library books and magazines. For example, you can make mobiles from wire coat hangers and cutouts from old Christmas cards. Glue on string to hold the three metal bars floating above each other.

🛋 Bake bread together.

🛋 Have a taffy pull.

🛋 Tape record family singing and interviews with each other and listen to them when you pull out the photo albums in the future. Send copies of the tapes to relatives you don't get to see very often.

🛋 As part of a family member's birthday, look at his or her photo album. Write in the album the cute, funny, amazing quotes that person says.

🛋 Research your family tree, interviewing and taping your oldest relatives about their parents and grandparents. See how far back you can trace your family history. Your local librarian may help you find the records.

🏃 Rent a video camera, write and direct a movie with your family and friends as actors.

🏃 Organize a block party in your neighborhood with potluck dinner and games. Organize a scavenger hunt, with clues to finding the next object.

🏃 Say tongue twisters like: She sells seashells down by the seashore; bushy Barry bear barely bakes berries; how many peppers could Peter Piper pick, if Peter Piper could pick peppers? and little Lizzie lazes in her lorry lately. Make them up with family members' names.

🏃 Play 20 questions, to figure out the animal, mineral, or vegetable object the other person has in mind.

🏃 Design a coat of arms for your family, using encyclopedia pictures to see how shields are designed.

🏃 Plant a vegetable and flower garden in pots or in your yard.

🏃 Have a family squirt gun, whipped cream, or jello fight.

🏃 Watch the clouds or stars together, describing what images you see.

🏃 Play games in the car, such as race to spot all the letters in the alphabet from signs or see who can find the most Volkswagen bugs ("slug bug").

🏃 Do a round robin story, where each person makes up a section as you go along.

🏃 Improvise a dialogue as actors, perhaps using accents.

🏃 Create your own plays or do charades.

🏃 Sing rounds and make up rap songs.

🏃 Copy the leader's hand clap or dance step until everyone gets it right.

🏃 Play noncompetitive "New Games" as well as sports.

🏃 Go skating.

♥ Go for a walk.

♥ Visit a museum.

♥ Write family letters to politicians urging them to support something you believe in, such as environmental cleanup, or write to protest ads you think are a bad influence.

♥ Watch funny videos together.

Read funny books out loud. These books are recommended by counselor Judith Eberhart: Robert Fulghum, *It Was on Fire When I Lay Down on It* , and *All I Really Need to Know I Learned in Kindergarten;* Robert Byrne, *The 637 Best Things Anybody Ever Said;* and Ashleigh Brillant, *I May Not Be Totally Perfect, But Parts of Me Are Excellent.*

Add to **family rituals** to celebrate the seasons and holidays. For example, in our family we backpack and make fruit pies in the summer, dress up for Halloween in the fall, watch migrating water birds and ski in the winter, and hike to wildflowers in the spring.

Ask each other some of the 260 questions in Gregory Stock's *The Kids' Book of Questions*, like, "If you could pick any one food and have nothing else during the next week, what would you pick?" or "Would you rather be a rich and famous movie star or a great doctor who saves a lot of people but is not wealthy or well known?"

A family I know has an instant party bag, containing balloons and streamers, to use when celebrating an achievement, such as a good grade on a test. They quickly pull out the bag at dinnertime when someone has an occasion to celebrate. Another family has a "family clap" where everyone applauds the speaker who tells about something that makes them proud. They also play the pen game, where the person holding the pen (microphone) is listened to by everyone else without interuption.

Weekly **family meetings** keep family communication healthy. Topics to be discussed can be written down on a list posted on the refrigerator as they come up during the week. All take turns being the leader of the meeting, including the young people. Start with what you like about each other. Include decisions such as where to go on a vacation or what to purchase for your home. Schedule fun times on your family calendar. Each person can have his or her own color of ink, with a color for the family as a whole. Family meetings should not be gripe sessions where people just complain or parents discipline, as no one will want to come. They should end with a fun activity like a favorite dinner, or pillow fight, or dancing, so that people look forward to them.

Journal Questions

1. List what you would like to do for fun with your family.
2. Ask other family members to make a list and see what you agree about doing. (It's a good idea to mark these times on your family calendar so they happen regularly.)
3. Draw how you're feeling now in your journal.

CHAPTER 6

GOING BACK AND FORTH BETWEEN TWO HOMES

Staying close to both parents often means you have two homes. Jayce reports:

It's a tough adjustment, but it gets easier. Always have something of your own at each house. The ideal is to stay at one house and have the parents switch. My mom had friends who tried it, but it was too much contact, like living together. Going back and forth can work if you live nearby, in the same city. Sometimes I didn't want to go over there, but my baby half sister kept me going over there a lot.

It's not convenient as you get older to be away from all your friends. In high school, I started not doing weekends at my dad's. It was hard when he moved to another city and I was cheerleading and spending time with my boyfriend. Parents should try to make things as stable as they can. My mom thought about moving to another state, before she met my stepfather. Things would have been so different.

I pretty much live with my mom, Chris explains, *but I see my dad every other weekend and three nights out of the week. I get less time. I feel lost and I want to have a whole family. The awkwardness of this is very intense. One day I just started the new plan and that was that. No questions asked.*

He suggests, though, if you go back and forth, "Be glad you see them. Try to put up with it or help them make a better situation. For six months, my dad had a new work plan so I didn't see him for a week at a time."

Chris doesn't like having to be shifted around and gathering up his homework papers when his dad picks him up on two school nights. It's a half hour drive each way, so it seems like he spends as much time in the car as at home. The current arrangement is that his dad picks him up at his mom's house and his mom picks him up and returns them to her house. His ideal plan would be to spend each weekend with his dad and the weekdays with his mom. He's suggested the idea to his dad but is afraid to bring it up with his mom.

After a divorce, young people are likely to **live with their mother** and see their father less often. "A plan that only allows you to see one parent two days out of every 14 days is awful," says Joel, but mothers seem to be awarded more time with their children. I agree with Joel that the idea of one parent becoming a visitor doesn't make sense and isn't fair.

In a study of two California counties by Dr. Eleanor Maccoby and others, two-thirds of the mothers had sole physical custody, 20 percent of the parents had joint physical custody, and nine percent of the fathers had sole physical custody. Similarly, in Dr. Joyce Arditti's study of divorced fathers in a Virginia county, 73 percent of the children were in sole mother custody, 22 percent had joint custody, and 5 percent had split custody, where some children were with the father and some with the mother. (See the definition of legal terms on page 123.)

Among our youth, 99 are with their moms most of the time, and of those, 27 lost contact with their dads. Fifty more also spend more time with their mom but see their father every other weekend or weekend days, and 41 live mainly with their father. Some switched from one parent's home to the other when they were in their teens. Only 31 have equal time with both parents.

My son has an equal relationship with his dad and me; I'm a great fan of shared parenting as being best for the children and parents, so I am disappointed that this arrangement is the least common. Generally, our experts got less time with their dad after the divorce; some got less time with both because their mom had to work more. A counselor in Seattle observes that, "Many children with 50/50 arrangements do not like them. It sometimes works for one sibling and not the other."

A Michigan school counselor also told me that many of his students don't like joint physical custody. He thinks it works only if the parents cooperate well; studies agree that the most damaging problem for kids is to be caught in their parents' conflicts. However, some researchers (see Joan Kelly, 1993, in the parent's bibliography) found that teens with two homes did better both in school and emotionally than teens who lived with just one parent. It makes sense that having the attention of two caring adults is helpful.

Some young people never see their fathers. They often miss him, feel hurt and angry about not seeing him, feel cheated and abandoned, feel they are missing something, or feel forgotten because their dad has a new family. "He has a new family and doesn't want to be bothered with me." Some feel that their custodial parent is jealous and pushes the other parent away. Over two million mothers do not have custody of their children, so this problem of the disappearing parent can include moms as well as dads. A few of our youth experienced this when their mothers moved out of state.

❧

Common sense would tell us that **kids usually succeed better with two supportive parents**, and studies back this up, as I showed in my book *50/50 Parenting*. Grandparents, aunts, and uncles used to help rear children, but people move so much now that kids may have just one main adult to care for them. Historically, this is unusual and difficult because it produces isolation and strain. Some studies report that kids do better with the same sex parent, so the fact that moms usually get physical custody may be harder on boys. However, studies are showing a "sleeper effect" for girls without involved fathers. As teens, they tend to search for male attention in early dating and sexual contact and Dr. Wallerstein found many of her female subjects had difficulty establishing committed relationships as young adults.

So it's wise for both sexes to do whatever they can to stay close to both their parents. Grandparents and extended family are important, too. Many kids who don't have close contact with both their parents do OK because they get love and support from their parent, grandparents, friends, brothers and sisters, teachers, their religion, pets, etc.

Most **younger children have no say** in the custody arrangement. Usually the parents decide, although in some cases the court makes the plan. About 41 states require judges to talk with kids to get their input into the custody arrangement; judges often privately interview children over seven or eight to hear their viewpoints, although none of our experts reported this. Our older youths are more likely to decide where they prefer to live. Overall, only a minority decide on their own living arrangement. Over the years after the divorce, many change the original arrangement, either switching to the other parent's home or spending less time with the noncustodial parent.

Our experts strongly advise **not to pick one parent**, because they feel torn and guilty about hurting the other parent. "If parents make the kids choose, I guarantee there will be resentment." An assertive nine-year-old boy who was asked by his counselor whom he wanted to live with answered; "I insisted on both. I stay three days with my dad and four days with my mom." Studies show that kids who are asked to select a custodial parent often pick the most needy parent, who may not be the best parent. "My mom leaned on me to stay with her," reported Eileen. Ideally, kids can stay close to both parents.

Arguments exist pro and con for **going back and forth** between two homes. Here are the **pros**.

🐂 "Joint custody is best. I couldn't imagine growing up without both my parents."

🐂 "Although I would have liked one home, I didn't want to stop seeing either parent."

🐂 "You won't have the same kind of closeness unless you see and talk to them every day."

🐂 "Be happy you have two parents who love you."

🐂 "Appreciate that both parents want to spend time with you. I hardly know my father."

🐂 "Make sure you get to know them; later in life you'll never really know who they are."

🐂 "Quality time is improved."

🐂 "There is a great sense of guilt when you choose one parent over the other."

🐂 "It can make you feel good because they tend to spoil you more and do fun things. You have twice the family."

Here are the **cons**.

🐕 It's a hassle, a bummer, hard, tough, confusing.

🐕 "Transitions are the hardest."

🐕 "My parents gave me the choice too often; moving around, having to readjust so often is rough."

🐕 "You forget stuff."

🐕 "I need one stable home, but keep visiting time up with the other parent."

❧ "The parent you're with always wants you to take their side in arguments between your parents."

❧ "Stability is important to kids, especially after the emotional loss of stability with a divorce."

❧ "It's hard packing up and being an hour away from your friends."

❧ "At a certain age friends become more important and then one must choose where he/she has good friends."

❧ "Going back and forth is forever a difficult issue, especially at holidays."

❧ "I would get sick to my stomach every time I went to my dad's for three weeks in the summer, because it was hard for me to adjust."

Advice for living in two homes emphasizes staying neutral, speaking up about your likes and dislikes, and making sure you have your own room (or at least some space you can call your own) at each house.

✹ "Keep an open mind."

✹ "Don't compare one parent to the other."

✹ "Don't confuse yourself with what your mom likes and what your dad likes. Stand on your own two feet and be proud."

✹ "Try to like both parents."

✹ "Don't do it for the parents." "Do what is best for you."

✹ "Tell each parent how you could make each house into a home."

✹ "Don't go to one to escape the authority of the other."

✹ "Never use one parent against the other."

✹ "Don't lie and say, 'Well, Mom/Dad lets me do this or that.'"

✹ "Try to explain that parenting should not be a popularity contest."

✹ "Enjoy the time you have."

✹ "Have fun in both homes."

✹ "It's almost like living a double life with two times the pets, friends, and family. Have fun with both lives and combine what you experience. Learn as much as you can from everything that happens."

🌀 "It's teaching you to get along with other parts of life because the rules are always different in any setting."

🌀 "Kids need to know that they have rights."

🌀 "It takes some organization. If they don't live near each other, that's their problem. It's their responsibility to get you back and forth."

🌀 "Don't tell what goes on in the other home." (Dr. Judith Bauersfeld comments that trying to keep secrets from a parent is damaging and parents shouldn't burden their kids with requests not to tell. It's wise to keep the two houses separate and parents shouldn't ask about what goes on in the other house.)

Several experts suggest if you feel too unsettled, try longer periods before switching to the other home, such as every two weeks, or every month, or every semester. Sometimes it's a hassle to go back and forth, but you get used to it, and it's worth it to stay close to both your parents.

Journal Questions

1. How do you feel about the living arrangement you're in now? What would be ideal for you? Have you discussed your ideas with your parents? Remember, they're divorced, but you're not divorced from them.
2. Have you tried any fun activities from the last chapter?
3. If you could go anyplace in the universe now, where would you visit for a week?
4. If you could go straight though the earth to the other side, where would you come up?

DRAWING BY CASEY FAY

CHAPTER 7

STAYING CLOSE TO BOTH PARENTS

Jayce and Luke had a tough time staying close to their father. Luke is intimidated by his dad and has trouble approaching him. Jayce says:

My father doesn't really know about the daily things of my life. He always came to my cheerleading and my brother's sports events in high school, until he moved. That was hard for him, so he distanced himself emotionally, too. Now that I'm in college, sometimes he doesn't ask, so I don't tell, except things where I've succeeded because he expects a lot of me.

I took a counseling class and decided to write to him to let him know I felt we weren't close and I needed a father, but he wasn't around, wasn't calling me. He called and said he is always very proud of me, but has a hard time expressing it, because his parents never told him. He had communication problems with his father, too. It's been a 1,000 times better since I wrote that letter. I was completely honest. Go for it, you have nothing to lose. (Luke doesn't have the strength yet to approach him.)

Chris says, "Sometimes I want to go with my dad, but I also love my mom." He doesn't like having less time with both his parents, but doesn't have the problem of one parent dropping out. His parents have joint legal custody, with physical custody to his mother, a common decision of the courts. His dad's lawyer discouraged him from even asking for physical custody because he thought the courts favored mothers.

∽

Overall, the main problem facing young people after divorce is that too often **a parent without custody fades out of the picture**. Because moms get custody most of the time, the disappearing parent is usually the dad. Studies find that one-half to two-thirds of children and fathers keep in regular contact after divorce, according to Professors Ahrons and Miller. One-third is still too many fathers and their children missing out on that special relationship. Carrie reports, "I feel like part of me is missing because I never had a male role model, even though my mom did a good job on her own."

Studies show that **lack of contact between father and child can create problems**, especially obvious for boys. But researchers suggest that girls don't act out the same way as boys and may not show the effects of divorce until they start dating. Some studies suggest that girls raised without their dads get boy-crazy as teenagers, searching for attention from males in a way that may not be wise. Katie says, "My life probably would have been a lot more stable if I had a male influence and known how to relate to men better."

Because moms without physical custody may also lose touch with their kids, everyone involved needs to make a special effort to make the noncustodial parent feel wanted. (This is why some are in favor of joint custody to keep both parents involved.) "Children often feel angry with their noncustodial parent," Brent reports. I urge those young people to talk about their feelings and include praise for both parents when possible. Another of our experts advises sending cards to remind your father how much he means to you.

Here's a list showing what different researchers found about the percent of fathers who stay involved after divorce. I'm including this list because I think keeping fathers involved with their children is one of the most important family issues of our time, beat out only by poverty (one in five children in the U.S. is poor). The two issues are connected because involved fathers are more likely to pay child support. The list also shows that social science is inexact. (The authors' articles and books on the topic are found in the parents' bibliography; the date in the list is the date of publication.)

Fathers' Involvement After Divorce:

🐎 Maccoby, 1993: 66% of fathers are involved.

🐎 Ahrons & Miller, 1993: 75% have contact at least twice a month, five years after the divorce; children average 2 to 3 nights a month at their dad's home.

🐎 Hetherington, 1993: 20% have contact once a week or more, almost one-half are not involved 11 years after the divorce.

🐎 Kelly, 1993: average time with father is 30% of the child's time.

🐎 Kruk, 1992: half of fathers are involved.

🐎 Arditti, 1992: 79% have contact at least twice a month, 13% are not involved.

🐎 Phares, 1992: in mother-custody homes, 19% have weekly contact, 42% some, 35% no contact.

🐎 Seltzer, 1991: 89% are involved.

🐎 National Commission on Children, chaired by Senator John Rockefeller, 1990 (900 children ages 10 to 17): a third see their fathers at least once a week, nearly 20% no contact.

🐎 Healy, 1990: two-thirds have contact at least every two weeks.

🐎 Pasley & Ihinger, 1989: one-half are involved.

🐎 Seltzer, 1988: 89% are involved.

🐎 Haskins, et al., 1987: 40% have weekly contact, 19% not involved.

🐎 Weitzman, 1985: 63% have more than weekly involvement, 23% not involved.

🐃 Furstenburg, 1983: one-third see their children more than once a month, 35% no involvement.

🐃 Zill, 1983: 25% of children in stepfather families have involved fathers.

🐃 National Survey of Children, 1976-1981: 27% have contact at least once a week, 44% not involved.

Professor Terry Arendell interviewed 75 divorced fathers in New York to find out why some of them drop out. He found out that fathers often withdrew to end conflict and power struggles with their former wives. One of the absent fathers Dr. Arendell interviewed explained, "I will not be a visiting uncle. Until and unless I can be a father in every sense, I simply refuse to have any part of this..... Our rights as fathers are simply negated, erased [by the courts]." Another father said, "Seeing my children simply reopens old wounds." A study by Jack Wall also found that absent fathers were often trying to avoid hostility with their ex-wives.

Counselor Steve Flowers observes that men are taught they should be the head of the family, having the last word, as in "Wait until your father gets home," or "Ask your father." If the mother has physical custody of the child, the father feels uncomfortable and "he'd rather be on top somewhere else." Even though it's almost the twenty-first century, old ideas about sex roles are still stuck in our minds.

Just as there is prejudice against women in high–powered jobs, there is a **bias against fathers**, a belief that children need their mothers more than their fathers. The movies "Kramer vs. Kramer" and "Mrs. Doubtfire" illustrate fictional cases where the courts were biased toward the mothers. In "Parenthood," Helen complains that, "Your father left to party and I stayed to raise two kids" who search for male contact. Steve Martin's character tries hard, but work competes for his attention. This is an interesting film to spark your thinking about fathers' roles.

Young men don't get as much experience taking care of little kids and aren't likely to read magazines that teach about parenting skills. If you're a male, you might want to consider taking a parenting class and doing some babysitting so you get around the bias against men caring for little children.

Men are considered amateurs at parenting, while women are thought of as professionals. Judges and other authority figures often expect that kids will spend more time with their mothers. Many dads tell me that people think of them as "babysitting" their own kids, or strangers give them advice about how to care for their kids, as if only mothers really can take care of children. People make fun of "Mr. Mom" as if only women can run a house. You might want to see the video of that title to check out the gender biases.

Here's an example of prejudice against fathers in a 1988 children's book *Why Are We Getting a Divorce?* by Peter Mayle. One picture shows a sweating father trying to iron: his son is looking down at his shirt, scorched with an iron-shaped burn. The text explains,

> *Your mother, even if she works at a job outside of the home, is probably still a lot better at looking after you and your home than your father is. Mothers usually are. Your dad may be a great cook and a whiz at doing the ironing, but most fathers aren't.*

Another example in an otherwise fine book for fathers to fill-in for their children. *Dad Remembers*, by Judith Levy, has the father saying, "Alone in the kitchen, I can rustle up some grub. But when it comes to cleanup, I hate to clean and scrub," as if somehow women like to cleanup and men don't. The truth is probably that nobody really likes to clean-up and, since it is simple work, we are equally capable of doing it.

Like most prejudices, the facts don't support beliefs that women are better parents. There is no parenting instinct, as studies of monkeys raised without a mother show; they only know how to care for a baby if they have watched a mother at work. Otherwise new monkey mothers are clueless and neglectful. Good parenting is learned and men are as capable of learning as women. The kinds of nurturing and teaching skills used by good parents are also used by male teachers, counselors, doctors, ministers, priests, and rabbis. Women don't have a monopoly on the human ability to love, and our society does something very wrong to discourage men from staying close to their children after divorce.

If parents are fighting, sometimes one of them feels it would be best for the kids to end the conflict by ending contact with the other parent. The other parent may feel so frustrated about not being able to see the child enough that he or she just gives up to end the pain of separation/union/loss. The pain of short contact followed by good-byes may be too much to bear. Sometimes the custodial parent is so angry at the other one that she or he makes excuses for why the kids can't see the other parent or tries to make the kids feel guilty if they see him or her. Sue tells us,

> *My mom uses visiting my dad as a punishment to me, so I go there upset. I think mothers play a big role in the relationship between distant fathers and their children. My stepdad's ex-wife destroyed the relationships he had with his sons. There should be a law that prohibits mothers and fathers from interfering in parent-child relationships.*

I asked Bob, one of my older students, why he doesn't see his sons from his first marriage. He was a firefighter who took care of the boys on his days off work, so he was close to them and an involved father. During the divorce, the two attorneys met with the judge for an hour. When Bob's attorney came out, he said, "If you believe in prayer, you had better start praying because the judge does not like us. He is pro-mother." Bob gave up contact with his boys after a session with a therapist who asked the oldest son if he wanted to see his dad. "All he could do was look at the floor, cry, and say no. The therapist's statement still tears out my heart." He said, " Every time after a visit with you their mother would tell them if they had fun they were going to hell because you are the devil, so it is harmful to their well-being to see you."

I asked Jon Luvaas, a lawyer, mediator, and divorced father, why we have a problem with fathers fading away after divorce. His ex-wife moved to another city, so he too did not get to spend a lot of time with his sons. Mr. Luvaas explains that our culture de-emphasizes the role of the father, and both dads and moms buy into this thinking. Because men usually earn more than women, they spend more time at work, and women spend more time at home with children. The courts recognize history rather than hope; even if the dad wants to get more involved after divorce, the court is likely to give him just every other weekend and alternating Wednesdays with his kids. Courts can lock parents into continuing the pattern of the mother spending more time with the children. The child then feels as though she or he is being rejected, feels hurt and angry, and pulls away, making the gulf between them wider.

Mr. Luvaas believes that it's a killer combination to set up mom as the sole custodian, who controls when dad sees his kids, and then asks dad to pay child support. Men tend to believe that their ex-wives benefit from the money rather than the kids and they feel manipulated and powerless. She's in a position to pull a lot of strings and may try to push him away from the kids to punish him or because it's upsetting to see him. It's understandable that in this kind of no-win, frustrating situation, a dad will back off, even though he loves his children.

As a **mediator** working with parents to decide on custody arrangements, Mr. Luvaas encourages parents to understand each other. Divorcing couples are often angry, afraid of being controlled by their ex-partner, and afraid of the unknown future. Power and control issues are almost always present and they lead to wrong assumptions. For example, Mr. X often shows up late to mediation meetings. Ms. X assumes he's being inconsiderate to her or trying to irritate her. He doesn't know that it matters to her that he be on time. They need to check out their assumptions.

Jon Luvaas tries to help parents arrive at win/win arrangements by talking and listening to each other to gain understanding. He suggests that Mr. X repeat back what Ms. X said, and vice versa, to make sure they really understand each other. His advice to kids is to talk to their parents and others about their feelings until they feel understood. They may need to say, "This is important, but I don't feel like you're listening to me." Kids with self-respect do the best in getting through divorce, he finds.

Many young people have a problem keeping close to both parents after divorce. If this becomes a problem for you, what can you do about it? John reports that lack of frequent contact with his father "scarred me because I feel that he just gave me money and I never went to see him." Gordon Clay, a divorced father and director of the National Men's Resource Center in San Francisco, suggests that **kids tell their dad, "I love you**. I want to spend time with you, not spend your money. I don't have to be entertained. Help me with my homework or. . ." Ask your dad to be, not do, Mr. Clay suggests.

Dads hear, "I need money for shoes" more often than "I love you," he reports. Ask your father about how he and his father grew up. Because men are taught to buy love with things money can buy, such as flowers, candy, jewelry, or toys, the provider role can get in the way of closeness between fathers and kids.

Several books give ideas about how distant parents can stay in touch with their children. George Newman suggests *101 Ways to Be a Long Distance Super-Dad*, including scheduled phone times and exchanging tapes. Singer Dwight Twilley finds that sending his daughter fun questionnaires keeps them close. His book *Questions from Dad: A Very Cool Way to Communicate with Kids* gives many delightful examples of his questionnaires. His daughter Dion writes questionnaires for him too and they even write them for their pets.

How to Write Questionnaires to Stay in Touch

Mr. Twilley suggests 100 categories of questions about school, friends, pets, hobbies, dreams, food, entertainment, sports, holidays, heroes and villains, fads, nature, travel, and jokes.

Questions can take many forms, including: true or false, multiple choice, yes or no, which is best, fill in the blank, name things (such as a home video we can make), put a symbol (a heart, a happy face, a sad face) in the box, make lists (your favorite foods), and challenges (write your name the best you can and the worst you can). Requests for drawings are fun, too, such as draw an alien from Mars, or the fleas' Christmas parade, or complete squiggles.

A parent can include photographs, along with a self-addressed stamped envelope and should resist the impulse to correct the child's spelling and grammar, Mr. Twilley concludes.

How to Stay Close to Both Parents

Use the problem-solving list of questions on page 14, and get information from school counselors, teachers, clergy persons, librarians, and court mediators. Use good communication skills to make yourself heard. Use assertiveness techniques of repeating politely and firmly what you need. Usually this means deciding on a clear statement of what you want and repeating it firmly and calmly, like "I need both my parents. Some Africans say it takes a whole village to raise a child. I need at least my two parents."

Write letters so you'll be understood, starting with positive statements about what you love about your parent. Frequently call your other parent to let him or her know how important he or she is to you, exchange audio and video tapes, questionnaires, and use computer networks to write to each other if you have access to them.

In dealing with a stepparent who might discourage closeness with your parent, apply the Bible's golden rule of doing to others as you want done to yourself. Often this applies to the stepmother. Ask, "How would you like it if your kids lost contact with their dad?" Or, "How would you feel about losing touch with your father?" Tell the stepparent it's not an either/or situation. A good relationship with you will make your dad feel happier and that's good for her and her kids, too. It can be magical to sit down and really listen to each other instead of building walls that increase separation and misunderstanding.

Journal Questions

1. What do you appreciate about your father? Your mother?
2. In what ways are you similar to each of your parents?
3. What do you wish you knew about each parent's childhood that you haven't yet asked about? Ask.
4. Think about how to get to know more about each parent as if you are writing a newspaper story about them.
5. Can you plan more time to communicate with the parent you know least about?
6. What's your most embarrassing moment?
7. Have you ever laughed so hard you cried? Why?

CHAPTER 8

DEALING WITH YOUR PARENTS' DATING AND REMARRIAGE

Jayce cried when her parents remarried within a few months of each other. In her dad's home, her stepmother "tries to make everything good for my dad and me and my brother. We probably would hardly have had a relationship with my father if he had married a woman who didn't like us. My stepmom made sure we had our time with Dad." In her mom's home, Jayce says Bruce and her mother are a match made in heaven. They tell each other how they feel and do things together they enjoy, like going camping. They respect each other.

But Jayce and Bruce fought:

The biggest adjustment was a new home, a new parent, and a new sister. I'm strong-willed, it's tough to have someone tell me I can't do something I've always done. He's sometimes authoritarian. I'd talk to my mom with an attitude and he didn't like that. We fought a lot and I wanted to be with my stepmother while she was pregnant and had the baby. It hurt my mom a lot when I moved out in my freshman year. It took that year for me to see Bruce is a wonderful person. His daughter is like my sister. My stepdad is more of a father figure to my brother and they have mutual interests.

Chris wasn't happy about his parents starting to date, either:

I felt second. I really didn't have as much attention as before.

I was lonely. When my dad remarried. It's nice having a stepmom but I don't feel as free to talk to her or my dad when she is around. And because I am not her child, I don't feel good enough for her. Everyone has good parts, you just have to find them.

In the beginning, Chris thought:

"Who is coming into my house? A stranger." I judged her too fast because my mom thought she was the person who broke up the marriage. This helps me not to judge people now before I know them. She is a pretty nice person and we like the same stuff, like walks. Dad didn't go on walks before.

I asked Chris what he would think about having a half brother or half sister. He hadn't thought about it, but said it would be one more person to take on walks and stuff. "Rebecca and I had our dad all to ourselves before Margaret came, it was like taking half of my dad away. A baby would be another chunk of Dad that would be taken away, but it would be an interesting experience. I like babies."

When their parents start dating, most young people report feeling jealous, protective of their parent, alienated, left out, weird, icky, upset, angry, resentful, hating it, or fearing they were losing attention. Some say they threw tantrums, freaked out, made fun of the dates behind their backs, and played practical jokes on them. Some feel OK about their mom dating and not their dad or vice versa, depending on how soon she or he started dating, whom they dated, and what effect it had on time with the child.

Some of our experts are happy if their parents are happy: " Dating was "like a beam of happiness hit them," but these young people are in the minority. If you feel jealous or upset when your parents start to date, you're normal. Seventy-five percent of divorced mothers and 80 percent of divorced fathers remarry within three to five years, so it's likely that you will experience dating and stepfamily life. Some of the experts' parents don't date or remarry, but they are in the minority.

When your parents start going out with new people, this is another stage in the divorce process that usually **starts out to be difficult** but gets better. Dating is a reminder that your parents really are not going to get back together and it shifts their attention away from you. Some young people like the new adults in their life, but it can be hard when you don't like the friend or you don't respond to each other well. Practice your communication skills (active listening, "I" messages, suggesting specific solutions) to make your needs understood by your parents.

Tell your parent what would help you feel more secure, such as knowing that you will do one fun activity with just that parent each week or have a regular talk together before bed. You might need to politely tell the new person that you would be happy to be friends but you already have two parents. If possible, share any positive things you like about that person so she or he does not feel rejected.

☻ "It's painful but my parents are happier with new partners."

☻ "It's hard to accept a new person in your life when it should be your mother or father."

☻ "Dad went directly to another woman, which was hard to deal with. I kept comparing her to my mom."

☻ "I feel like he's trying to replace my dad and no one can ever do that."

☻ "I was much more receptive to my mom's boyfriends than my dad's girlfriends–none of them really stood a chance with me."

☻ "It's hard to accept a new person but I have learned a lot."

☻ "My mom dated a real slime when I was very young."

☻ "I felt like Mom was leaving me forever when she went out on a date."

☻ "I was scared because Mom went out late."

- "I felt lonely because I didn't get as much attention."
- "When my dad likes someone for a while it's like he forgets us kids."
- "I felt very uncomfortable. When Dad first had a woman spend the night, I was 16 and it shocked the hell out of me."
- "I felt I needed to protect my mother."
- "I won't let my mom get married."
- "When I was younger I wanted to have my mother to myself. Now I have a boyfriend and I just want my mom happy."
- "I didn't like babysitting when my mom went on dates."
- "My mom started dating this guy who was really nice to me. I liked him a lot but they stopped dating. I didn't want to get close to any of her new boyfriends because I didn't know how long they'd be around."
- "I hoped dad's girlfriend and mom's boyfriend would get together and Mom and Dad would get back together."

Rick suggests that, "If you don't like the new boyfriend or girlfriend, speak up and tell your parent. That's crucial as you might get stuck with someone you hate." However, whom ever your parent goes out with and remarries is an adult decision, just as your choice of friends is usually up to you.

~ ⁓

The National Survey of Children found that over one-third of the children in **stepfamilies** will experience another divorce, and 10 percent will experience three or more divorces. Some of our young people also had to go through a second or third divorce. "I was thrilled to have another "normal" family when my dad remarried. Too bad it was a very dysfunctional relationship and it wasn't long before I was back in therapy." One girl reports being spanked with a wooden paddle by her 200-pound stepfather (this can be child abuse and should be reported) and being treated poorly by his children. She was relieved when her mother got a second divorce.

Stepchildren report that stepparents can bring new love and happiness or they can be "bad news" as in the fairy tales. Some stepparents are jealous or unfriendly or too strict. Some young people really enjoy their "nice" and "cool" stepparents. Our experts are slightly more likely to get along with their stepfathers than their stepmothers, as other studies also show. As one said, "I think my stepfather is great. He's really good to my mom. My stepmother likes to have my father all to herself so we don't see her much." But almost as many don't get along with their stepfathers.

Difficult stepparents don't want their new partners to have two families and they try to come between parent and child, or they try to be a disciplinarian too soon. Dr. Judith Bauersfeld, of the Stepfamily Association of America, would like you to think about the stepparent's point of view. Usually "difficulty comes from some frustration or confusion on their part." She encourages you to talk about the kind of relationship you would like, so that people understand each other's point of view. Being a stepparent can be hard and she asks that you think about what it's like for him or her.

Wendy Geis-Rockwood, who wrote the curriculum for "Shapes" groups for changing families, suggests that if you are having a hard time with a stepparent, speak up about how you feel. A parent's remarriage may trigger the stages of grieving you first went through during the separation, as it reminds you that your parents are not going to get back together. Some kids think if they are obnoxious, they can get rid of the stepparent, but that is not going to bring their parents back together.

Because some of the youth are so critical of "witchy" stepmothers, I talked with Margaret, Chris' stepmother, to hear about her experience. She said:

*It's been really tough for me because the children were pro-
grammed to hate me, to think that everything I do is bad.
Their mom told them never to kiss me and that I was the woman
who took their dad away, which is not true. I had no idea how
hard it would be, being manipulated by a person outside my
home. She phones here frequently and argues with my husband, sometimes three calls in one night.*

*The kids are very protective of her. Chris and his sister are
under a lot of pressure from their mother not to have fun here,
so they'd tell her they didn't enjoy it here. We weren't sure
when they were pretending because they were trying to please
everyone. Now we talk about it openly. It seems like children
of divorce have to learn that parents don't always tell the
truth about the other parent. Kids have to form their own
judgments and be true to themselves.*

If you put yourself in Margaret's shoes, perhaps you'll have more
understanding of the difficult position of a stepparent. From the
stepfather's view, school counselor Tony Nethercott sees many families where the daughter worship her father as her hero. Even if he is
an alcoholic, the girl blames her mother when he leaves. He sees
girls who give their mothers and stepfathers a hard time and imagine
that their fathers can do no wrong. They resent the stepfather for
replacing their biological father in the home, even though the problem rests with their parents. It's much easier becoming a stepfamily
if the biological parents have a harmonious system for staying close
to both them.

Here are negative and positive reactions to having a stepparent:

⊕ "It is very awkward having another woman getting my father's
attention. We're not as close."

⊕ "My stepmother is very jealous of me and my mother; my dad and

I drifted apart."

⊕ "I resent seeing more of my stepfather than my own father."

⊕ "It's like having a new friend in the family that you are supposed to treat as a parent."

⊕ "My stepfather became my 'real' dad."

⊕ "The first time my future stepfather came to the house, I liked him right away and told my mom that she should marry him."

⊕ "When my dad got a girl friend, we got even closer."

Kriste was surprised when, after her parents' divorce, her mother moved in with her best friend as a lesbian couple. It took time for her to get used to this arrangement, but she likes her "stepmother" and that helps. About ten percent of the population in the United States is gay or lesbian, so you probably know people with this sexual preference, even if they are not open about it. The studies of kids with homosexual parents do not find they are more likely to be homosexual themselves or that their parents' sexuality has any effect on their ability to parent well. There are usually community support groups for families with gay or lesbian parents to provide more information, such as PFlag (Parents and Friends of Lesbians and Gays).

Stepfamilies are complicated. Kids are coming and going. There are ex-husbands and ex-wives, plus their parents, in the picture. Stepparents can be jealous of their mates' longer history with their kids, and kids can be jealous of attention to a new person. Kids who didn't grow up together may be expected to be like brothers and sisters. A family of two kids can expand to a blended family of six kids. A child who is an only child or the oldest can become the baby in the family.

Each family has its own rituals which may conflict with the other family's way of doing things. One family watches television at dinner, the other doesn't. This family opens Christmas presents on Christmas eve. The other one opens them on Christmas morning but only after breakfast, taking turns to open a gift, one at a time. How can these differences be resolved?

People may look at the stepfamily and expect it to be like a first marriage family or like the "Brady Bunch." This is an unrealistic expectation. Expectations are one of the biggest problems in relationships, especially if they are unspoken and no one talks about their disappointments and frustrations when their expectations are not met. It's much easier if you do not expect your stepfamily to be like your original family; otherwise, you'll be disappointed. If you expect a zebra and get a horse, you'll be sad. If you expect a horse and get one, you can handle it. Stepfamilies are, not better or worse, just different, explains Dr. Bauersfeld, who has much professional and personal experience.

Our experts advise that you try to enjoy having more family and friends, give the stepparent a chance, and realize that it takes time to get to know each other well. A frequent remark is that it takes time to get adjusted to a stepfamily, "because no one really knows how to act or react to everyday situations."

- "It's hard to adjust: Just try and get along."
- "Understand that it's all new to the stepparent, too."
- "Be tolerant."
- "Be patient with your stepparent."
- "Keep an open mind about a new family structure."
- "Be prepared for different philosophies."
- "It's more love to go around. Try to be understanding about how difficult it is for everyone to adjust to a new family situation."
- "It's hard at first. You feel like you have to do things to get attention from your real parent. It's hard to share your parent. But, after getting used to it, our stepfamily was great."

● "It's hard to bond like with a parent. Instead, be best friends with your stepparent on a special level."

● "Be honest with your parent. My stepmother would try to hurt me by saying my father didn't want me. This hurt very badly."

● "When a stepparent becomes controlling, which happens, you need to communicate and let them know that you are having a hard time taking rules. Build a respect that allows give and take."

Regarding stepsisters and stepbrothers, sometimes our experts enjoy having more family members and sometimes they compete. They suggest:

● "Get to be friends with your stepbrothers and stepsisters." "The problems mostly concern the kids. Sometimes we have a lot of fun together. Stepfamilies have a lot of ups and downs. It's never constant."

● Parents should "lay down rules for *all* the kids to follow instead of each side of the family following their own."

● Having a half sister or half brother can be fun: "I love being a big sis."

With all the complexities it means that good communication and conflict resolution skills are vital. I think every stepfamily can benefit from working with a counselor, even before they move in together. There are good books about stepfamilies, such as those by John and Emily Visher, therapists who live in a large stepfamily themselves and thrive. Stepfamily groups and newsletters are also available, such as through chapters of the Stepfamily Association of America.

Journal Questions

1. Which of the quotes above is closest to how you felt when a parent started dating? If they haven't started, how do

you think you'll feel if they do date?

2. What do you think it takes to make a stepfamily get to know each other well and cooperate? What do you observe in your friends' stepfamilies?

3. How do you feel about the possibility of getting stepsisters or stepbrothers?

4. What dramas are playing out in your dreams lately?

5. Can you name different parts of your personality, such as a comedian, a shy person, and a critical self? Are there movie stars that represent these personalities?

6. What's the best movie you've ever seen? Your favorite food?

7. If you could have any animal as a pet, what would you pick?

(In case you're wondering why I'm including questions that don't have to do with divorce, it's to take time to lighten up and get perspective.)

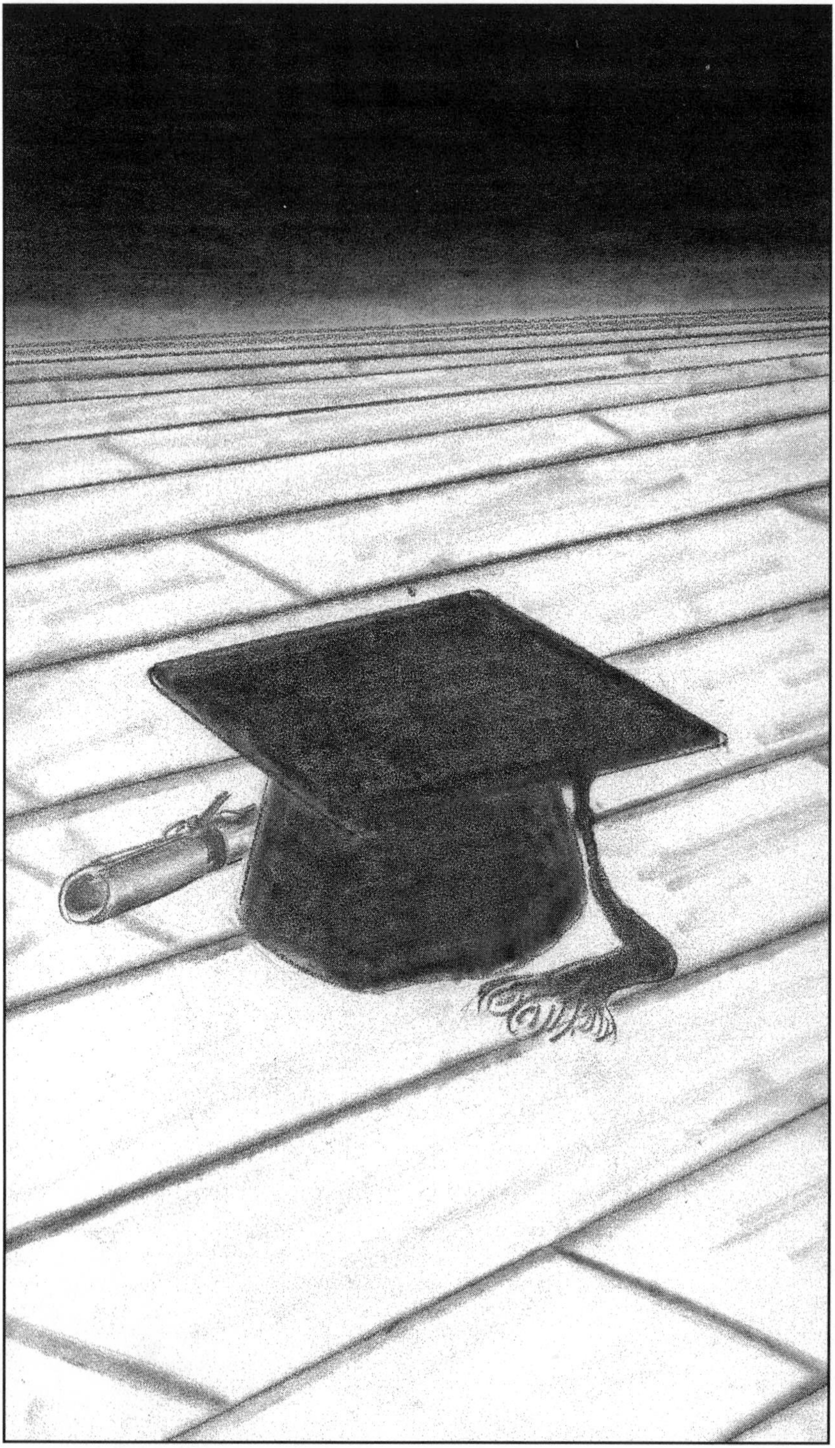

Drawing by Travis Crawford

CHAPTER 9

SCHOOL SUCCESS

Jayce and her stepsister are both "very good students." Jayce goes to a four-year university and Luke is in a community college. He hated school and found it hard to get motivated to study, but now he likes his college classes.

Chris reports he's an "A" student, which I believe, because he writes very well for a sixth grader. He thinks school is a lot of fun and is planning on continuing his education to become an environmental engineer. His sadness over the divorce hasn't affected his school success, but counselors I talked with report that grades drop for most kids following a divorce. They have difficulty concentrating while trying to sort out all their feelings. One of the counselors experienced the same thing when his wife died: "Your mind is so battered, it's hard to concentrate to read. " He froze emotionally and it took four years before he could work through his feelings and read books about coping with death.

This chapter provides tools for school success so you can keep on your path. I interviewed two teenaged boys, Joey and Jed, who went to a summer camp to learn the skills needed to succeed in school. Here's what they learned:

Get to know your **teachers'** interests and, if it fits, include their interests in your writing and conversation with them. Take time to stay after class and let a teacher know what you like about the class and about your goals. (As a teacher, I do pay more attention to students who talk to me about their goals for the course.) Sit in the middle or in the front (picture an upside-down "T") and make eye contact with the teacher, as students who sit in this "T" zone tend to do better. Don't sit where you can easily look out a distracting window or near a talkative friend. Take notes so that you concentrate on what the teacher is saying and don't space out. Always carry your calendar with you to immediately record in one place when assignments are due and other events.

To **memorize** information, associate it with something you know. Take the first letter of each word to memorize (such as the names of human bones or state capitals) and make up a sentence with those letters. Or picture them on different parts of your body, from head down to feet. Your brain learns by stimulating various senses, using pictures, sounds, and feelings. For example, let's say you want to learn the presidents of the United States. Starting with Washington, think of a noisy washing machine on your head and a ton of laundry. This helps you remember that he is the first president, and utilizes your senses of sight and hearing. To remember Jefferson as the second president, you might think of Jeff and his son, looking into your two eyes. For our third president, Monroe, you might think of three perfumed Marilyn Monroes sitting on your nose.

Jed and Joey asked me to give them a list of words to remember; I gave them random names, dates, animals, etc. They used this body-part memorization technique, and months later could still list the facts in the order I gave them, starting with the top of their head. We have different ways we learn and remember. Some of us learn best by seeing, some by hearing, and some by touching. Your school counselor might give you a learning style test so that you can know your strengths.

To take **tests** well, Joey and Jed learned to start with a deep breath from their lower stomach area. Quickly imagine the most calm and perfect place for you, such as a beach, a lake, a mountain top, or a sand dune. Look at the teacher for a moment to focus and then get started. Read the instructions carefully. Tilt the paper so your head is not bending over in a tired position. Go through the questions and do the easy ones first. When in doubt, go with your first response. Then go back to the questions you're not sure about. If you have time, check over the answers several times before handing in the test.

When answering an essay question, first make an outline to support your theme. To think up points to prove your theme, try "clustering," drawing a circle with the main topic inside. Then draw lines radiating from the circle, like a starfish, labeling them with ideas to support or prove your main idea. Do this quickly, without judgment: Just brainstorm. Do the outlining or clustering ideas directly on the test paper so your teacher can see that you know how to organize.

The first paragraph should tell the reader what you are going to write about, why, and the main points you will provide to prove your thesis. Then develop the points you've listed in the introduction in the body of the essay. In your conclusion, summarize the most important points and suggest what might develop in the future.

If assigned a **research paper**, first find a quidebook in your library, such as Phyllis Cash's, *How to Write and Develop a Research Paper*, or *The Term Paper* by Charles Cooper and Edmund Robins. Make sure you are absolutely clear on the assignment. I sometimes have to mark down my students' research papers because they didn't pay attention to the directions, as when they focus on describing a problem rather than on solving it, as I ask them to do.

Take notes for research papers on index cards. It takes too much time to try to organize notes with many points on notebook paper. Use only one topic per index card. List on the card the last name of the author and page number you are reading, and the theme number. For example, if you write a paper on the achievements of the Civil Rights movement, school integration could be theme one, equal opportunity to use public facilities like drinking fountains could be theme two, and so on.

When finished with all your reading, divide the cards into piles. Then organize the first topic's theme cards into an order that makes sense to you, use them as your outline, and write. If you read your essay out loud to yourself or a family member, you'll be able to hear where the paper needs more explanation or connection between ideas. A high school composition teacher told me to write essays for someone stupid, to explain the connection between ideas that may seem obvious to the writer.

∿∿∿

At home, make your senses happy to sit down and **study** by having a neat space, a beautiful picture, a favorite photograph, unbuttered popcorn to eat, juice to drink, relaxing background music, and a chart to check off your accomplishments. It's normal to think of excuses to avoid studying, such as you really need to clean your room or make a call, but stick to your schedule. Once you get started, you'll get on a roll. Sometimes it's best to start with your easiest assignment, because finishing it gives you the sense of accomplishment to go on to the next one. Usually it's best to do your hardest homework first, though, when your concentration is strongest.

When you read for schoolwork, always take notes because, just like listening in class, it's easy to space out if your body isn't involved in the activity of writing. Give yourself rewards; when I concentrate well for 20 minutes, I take a break to do what I want. Well, usually it's to do the dishes or pick up, but variety is the spice of life.

The **worst enemy** of school success is procrastination, saying to yourself, "I'll do it later." Putting off doing work robs you of energy and confidence, and makes the task you've put off seem twice as hard. In contrast, getting a job done adds to your energy and confidence. Break a big task into small daily parts. For example, if you have a report due, read about the topic for a half hour each day after dinner. Set aside a regular time and place to do homework.

Negative **self-talk** is another enemy, so post positive messages around your work space, such as "I am capable of deep concentration to remember what I read." Set realistic goals and reward yourself for achieving them, as we respond to rewards and praise. You might ask your parents to add to your rewards when you achieve a goal.

I asked Billie Jackson, head of the Student Learning Center at California State University, Chico, the **difference between an "A" and a "C" student**. (She has first-hand experience with her daughter and son, who graduated from UCLA and the University of California at Berkeley and went on to graduate schools.) "A" students start ahead of time; they don't cram for tests the night before. They do more than just the minimum requirements. They talk about what they're learning, putting new vocabulary to use. Organization is the key. They write down assignments in one place and have a notebook with sections and pockets for each subject.

Ms. Jackson observes that effective students have a study schedule. This involves a quick preview of the text and class notes before class, concentrating in class, and asking questions to prevent daydreaming. Review as soon after class as possible in a Sunday through Thursday scheduled homework time, with intensive review the night before a test. The key is to review information three to four times a week.

She suggests that you try a reading strategy called SQ4Rs (for the letters which begin each technique) when you read a text.

How to Read Effectively

❧ First quickly *survey* the headings, bold type, charts, and questions at the back of the chapter to create memory hooks. The main idea of each paragraph is usually in the first sentence. Ask yourself *questions* as you read each section. Answer these questions after *reading* each section, *recite* the answers out loud to use your various senses, and *record* your key answers in your notebook, then *reflect* by tying in the new information with what you already know. (You might want to take a speed reading workshop to learn how to increase your comprehension as well as speed.)

To improve your test-taking results, be overprepared and avoid cramming. Try to predict test questions as you study and write down answers on study cards. Breathe, relaxing your muscles as you exhale all your air, gently expanding your belly as you breathe in air. Do this at least three times. Ms. Jackson also suggests always reading the directions completely, noting point values so you can plan your time. Don't leave any answers blank, even if you have to guess. In true and false tests, inclusive words like "all" and "always" often flag a "false" statement. There are usually more true than false questions on a test. Longer questions are likely to be correct. Read multiple choice statements noting whether each is a "T" or an "F" so that you can respond to an "all of the above" choice (these are likely to be true).

Another important part of school, besides teachers and tests, is **friends**. A teenager who considers himself popular says his secrets of success are to risk getting to know strangers, listen well to people and ask them questions so they know you are interested in them, have the courage to be yourself, pick friends who like you for who you are, and don't discriminate against unpopular students. Liking yourself is important if you expect other people to like you. Being confident without being conceited is attractive, so practice your self-esteem techniques and keep adding to your journal list of qualities you like about yourself.

Observe well-liked and respected students to see what they do. But quality is more important than quantity of friends. Depending on their personality type, some people are happier with a few good friends while others like to meet and greet many friends. One style is not better than the other.

Since school success is linked to your career success in the future and to how you feel about yourself now, experiment with the techniques in this chapter to see which ones enhance your school performance.

Journal Questions

1. What are your favorite subjects?
2. Which subjects are hardest for you? Does your school have tutoring services?
3. What are your goals for school achievement this semester?
4. What is your plan for achieving these goals?
5. Do you have a study schedule? Rewards for sticking to it?
6. If you were going to become a teacher tomorrow morning, what subjects and grades would you want to teach?
7. Who is your favorite teacher of all time?
8. How did you feel your very first day of school? (I walked out.)
9. If you feel intimidated by someone, have you tried imagining them in his or her underwear?
10. If you had to live in a different historical period, which one would you choose?

CHAPTER 10

YOUR FUTURE

Jayce and her boyfriend have been going together for the past five years. She thinks he is someone she could spend the rest of her life with, although she has "fear in the back of my mind" about getting divorced. He's like her father in that sometimes he has a hard time seeing the positive, but he's the opposite of her father in not being concerned about material things and spending money. Her boyfriend plans to be a teacher, and is "a very caring person, making sure everyone is OK."

Chris reports, "I will still get married, but I will wait for the perfect person. My parents got married when they were young and stupid. This way I won't hurt my kids. If I know it won't work, I won't have kids. I'm a little more afraid of women than I was before because my mom favors my sister." When his parents were still married, he didn't know his parents' constant fighting wasn't normal. Now he sees that his dad and stepmother never raise their voices at each other. If they disagree, they talk about it, showing him it's much better to talk than to yell.

A school divorce group in Michigan chose this as the chapter they most wanted to discuss in their group. They focused on the need to compromise, recognizing that their parents' fighting is really hurtful. I asked one of their counselors, Tony Nethercott, about his advice for your future. He wants you to know that you can determine your path. Search for a vision and look for heroes to inspire you and show you how to succeed. Gina agrees, "It's important to know who you are, where you are going, and where you want to go in the future." ❊ What are your plans for the next five years?

Mr. Nethercott points to books such as comedian Andy Andrew's *Storms of Perfection.* He uses *Dave's Way,* by Dave Thomas, the founder of Wendy's restaurants, to show that people can succeed despite difficult childhoods. Dave's adoptive mother died when he was a baby, and his father did not provide a stable family life for him. But his grandmother gave him the support and caring he needed to do well.

What most young people learn from their parents' divorces is to **wait to marry** until they know their partner well and to learn to be a good communicator who knows how to work out problems. Most of our experts plan to get married and look forward to it.

● "I now realize a relationship is much like a beautiful garden. The more you work, the better it gets. But once you stop, it starts to die."

● "Kids who grew up through a divorce have spent a lot of time thinking about the problems that marriages face today."

● "I can't wait. I will work harder than my parents did."

● "I can't wait to feel like a dad, totally set financially."

● "I feel very positive. I know what to look for and won't make the same mistakes."

An exception to the plan to wait is Jacque, who at 20, is already married. She explains that she was "looking for the love and security that I felt I missed as a child."

Only 15 of the experts say they don't plan to get married, although two of those said they want to have children. Some are scared about marriage, commitment, and the possibility of divorce, as are many young adults today, even if their parents are still married.

● "I'm more cautious, afraid to commit, and I keep a lot to myself."

● "It makes me wonder if people need a practice marriage."

● "I have trouble trusting that marriage can last, but I want mine to, if I can find someone crazy enough to marry me."

● "It scares me but I will put in my all and not give up."

Some mention the **possibility of divorce**:

● "I hope it will be till death do us part. I hope if we do divorce, it will be civil."

● "I hope I don't repeat my parents' mistakes, but realistically, I probably will. I think I'm affected for life."

● "I don't think it's possible to prevent divorce altogether."

● "Marriage is a strong and valuable commitment, but not one you are destined to stay in. People change. If you aren't happy, you have every right to get a divorce, although it should be the last resort."

● "Divorce can be a practical means to get out of an unhealthy relationship. It's not a shameful thing."

Our experts emphasize the value of keeping communication lines open and working out problems. (In a survey of over 200 employed parents done by my students and me, they agreed that communication is the most important factor in a good marriage. They also mentioned respect, trust, being good friends, commitment, having a sense of humor, and having enough money to avoid stress.) Our experts mention the importance of not marrying too young, having a long courtship, learning from their parents' mistakes and of discussing everything before marriage, perhaps with a counselor's help. They plan to be very picky in selecting a faithful best friend with common goals as their spouse.

Rianna suggested that I "give people hope to have a good marriage and not everyone gets a divorce." Some of my college students believe that their parents are very happily married because they communicate well, are best friends, are loving, spend time together, respect and support each other, give and take, and work at the marriage.

- **O** "They work together, they see eye to eye."
- **O** "They still hug, kiss, and flirt together."
- **O** "They know that marriage takes a lot of work."
- **O** "They compromise."

▦ Think about good marriages you've seen, perhaps friends', parents', or relatives'. What do you like about these happy marriages? What keeps their marriages alive, happy, and close?

How to Have a Good Marriage

🐾 Adults with satisfying marriages I've interviewed for previous books emphasize they are best friends. They plan fun time together: Bonding is based on the shared memory of good times. They discuss conflicts and misunderstandings before molehills become mountains. They learn not to "gunny sack," stuffing little irritations in a bag until they build up and explode. This requires taking the risk of rejection or feeling petty, to talk about resentments, fears, irritations, jealousies, etc.

Couples have to schedule enjoyable time together, especially when they are busy with work and kids.

☬ Lisa reports, "You can always tell when my parents need more alone time, as there is more strain and it's not nearly as comfortable."

☬ Gina says, "When my parents are happy and at peace with each other, there is nothing that we can't get through." Remind your family of this important fact and contrast it with Larissa's story:

● "My parents put my sister and me before themselves. They put more time and effort into our happiness than into their relationship and now as a result they are not very close."

To sum up, youths report that separation, divorce, and parents' dating and remarriage are very difficult but usually get better with time. They are learning to be strong, to be adaptable, and to understand what it takes to make a marriage and family healthy. They intend to work hard in their future families.

Journal Questions

1. List the qualities of your ideal mate. Is your list realistic? Describe the best marriage you've seen.
2. List your strong points in your relationship with close friends and family members.
3. What do you want to learn and achieve before you settle down?
4. Describe a typical weekday in your life when you're 35.
5. What's your plan for the next year? Next five years? Next ten years?
6. What would you most like people to remember about you at the end of your life?
7. What does entering the twenty-first century mean to you?
8. What do you think you'd find if you time-traveled to your town 50 years from now?

DRAWING BY WALKER LEE

CHAPTER 11

FOR PARENTS

This section is especially for your parents; you may want to add your own suggestions in a letter or booklet. Included are summaries of young people's suggestions for parents and the psychological research about the effects of divorce on children. Jayce suggests that "parents should be open and communicative." Chris advises parents, "Just because your husband or wife has been mean to you, don't take it out on the kids because it will make them feel guilt. Don't yell at your kids."

A Summary of Youth's Advice for Parents

🐦 "There isn't a day goes by that I don't think about divorce. It's hard not knowing where one parent is. Just remember that if you bring children into the world, it's not just your life anymore, it's theirs you're messing with also."

🐦 Explain clearly why you divorced so that children understand they are not to blame. "Things were worse because I didn't know what was going on a lot."

🐦 Don't use your children as messengers or go-betweens, and especially not with the intent of hurting the other parent or spying on him or her.

🐦 Don't use your children as counselors or caretakers. You're the care-giver. Think about the kind of childhood they deserve. Find an adult counselor.

🦗 Develop an adult support system. Your child cannot fill in for your ex-spouse. A boy is not the man of the house, nor is a girl the housekeeper.

🦗 Listen to your children with full attention and without interruption, advice, or judgment. Spend some focused time with each one every day.

🦗 Don't criticize the other parent in front of the children. That person contributed half the child's genes.

🦗 Keep conflicts with the other parent away from the children.

🦗 A teacher/leader of support groups reminds parents that, "Your child is not a pawn."

Steve Flowers, a therapist who works with both adults and children and has experienced divorce himself, reports that many divorcing spouses engage in warfare and use their children for reconnaissance, an activity which is like a slow acting poison for the child. Usually one parent (or both) becomes far less available to the child, leading to abandonment fears and a damaged sense of self-worth and value. Children personalize the divorce, thinking they must have done something wrong. Children are especially suggestive during the trauma of divorce, so they should be protected from parental conflict and blame. Parents set the mold for how children relate to others.

He advises parents to make their children the focus of their life during the separation period to protect them from damage. He also suggests that codependent women (experts in enabling behaviors and establishing blind spots to overlook their husbands' abusive behaviors) break the cycle and not train their girls to do the same. Some angry women teach their boys that all men are bad, which leads them to conclude that they are bad too, and sometimes they act out this prediction.

Steve Flowers sees the effects of divorce continue into adulthood, explaining that children often feel rage and guilt when their parents divorce, and that if it isn't resolved, it seeps out through the cracks, later taking the form of addictions or punishing their spouses for the parents' failures. Blaming and condemnation don't hurt the object of the blame, but do harm the person carrying it around, as when manifested in health problems. As Mark, 21, wrote, "Don't try to hide your emotions. If you do, they will eat you up inside." (Although his parents divorced when he was 12, he reports that he still feels angry because his father moved out of state. He thinks, though, "it was better for them to get divorced when they did; otherwise, the result may have been catastrophic.")

Your child should be given the opportunity to have expert neutral guidance in sorting out feelings surrounding the divorce; if your insurance doesn't pay for counseling, check with the school district, religious groups, or the United Way about cost-free children's support groups.

Regarding the effect of divorce on children, a multitude of studies agree that **parents' conflicts damage children** if the children feel caught in the middle. It's painful for kids to hear their parents attack each other. If you must fight, do it when the kids are not around. Even better, resolve disagreements, and get on with your lives. Isolina Ricci, in *Mom's House, Dad's House*, suggests treating each other like business partners. You don't have to like each other, but should establish agreements and follow them. Counselor Lynne Reyman recommends that, "Everything possible should be done to avoid ongoing court battles which exacerbate the children's feelings of confusion, sadness, and loss." She agrees that high levels of hostility damage children, not the divorce per se.

On a personal note, after 13 years of switching my son Jed from mom's house to dad's house about every other night, I can testify that contact with Jed's father **gets easier**. Jed is with me Monday, Wednesday, every other Friday, and Sunday after noon. He's with me Christmas eve and his dad picks him up around 10 A.M. on Christmas day. We both attend his birthday parties and Thanksgiving depends on who has the most interesting plans. We're both free to travel, letting the other parent know as soon as plans occur.

The first year is hardest, because you and the other parent are likely to be angry, hurt, disappointed, upset about dating, and afraid of losing control over your kids. I felt intruded upon when Les, Jed's dad, came to pick him up and irritated when he was late. He soon got involved with a new woman and that added tension at first. My goal with both Les and Jed is to be fair and consistent rather than popular. I decided not to worry about what I can't control, such as what Jed eats or watches on TV at his other home. Now I feel like Les is a brother: I'm fond of him and we only mildly push each other's buttons, usually over the power and control issues common in most relationships. The bottom line is that we trust that each of us has the best interests of our son at heart.

I'm truly grateful for Les' wife, Donna, because she cares about Jed and is organized and dependable; I do most of the scheduling with her now. Jed is lucky to have three concerned parents. The three of us were talking together outside of Jed's school after a teacher conference and Jed pointed us out to his friends. He joked about being a "freak of nature" with three parents! Donna and I were at another conference where the person asked who was Jed's real mother. I said he has two moms. It certainly makes my life easier to share parenting.

I enjoy Jed more because I have breaks and I get writing like this done when he's at his dad's, and I can go out and travel without guilt about leaving him. Yesterday I told Jed he couldn't do something; he asked what would happen if he did, to see if it was worth doing anyway. I said I hadn't decided, I would like to consult with his dad. That did it. Having a back-up is a great help. Please think long-term about the advantages of sharing parenting, for the children and for you.

Cooperation is possible even between ex-spouses who fought when they were married. Pat, a divorced mother, took a parenting class with her ex-husband and his new partner so they could develop common ways of disciplining their shared children. These three co-parents stay in touch through phone conversations too. I wouldn't let anger nip a developing co-parent partnership in the bud.

I recommend to you that you share parenting even if you don't like the other parent or disagree with the way he or she does some things. That's life; you don't agree with all that school teachers do and kids cope with different styles of teaching. Studies report that mothers who share parenting are happier with the arrangement than mothers who parent solo. Fathers haven't been studied much, indicating the bias against them. Children are most satisfied in dual-residence arrangements (Maccoby, et al., 1993).

Studies consistently prove that children do better academically and socially with two parents, as described in *50/50 Parenting*. However, social science is inexact! Some studies do not find that continuing relationship with the noncustodial father makes a difference for the child's development. Fathers are more likely to stay involved and pay child support if they have joint custody, thus the advantages for every family member of shared custody (unless one parent is unfit) must be seriously considered.

If you can't bear to see your ex-spouse, then switch kids at lessons, school, or a friend's house. Negotiate a schedule with the help of a mediator, and then stick to it, so you don't have to talk to each other much about scheduling. Keep each other informed by writing notes if you don't even want to talk on the phone. Know that things will get better with time, as the kids report throughout this book. Forgiveness is a virtue, especially useful when strong feelings keep us attached to the past. It's best to lighten one's baggage and travel forward.

Judy Osborne, a therapist working with divorcing families in Boston, reports that, "I'm finding it more and more important to emphasize the maintenance of a mutually respectful parenting relationship in my work with divorcing couples." Her own kids experienced her divorce when they were 6 and 9 years old.

> *Their father and I have worked hard to maintain a parenting relationship and, as a consequence of that work, now enjoy our old friendship again. It has been important to our kids to have the regard and love still to demonstrate that they were wanted and that our relationship prior to their birth had enriching aspects for both of us.*

She also emphasizes the importance of helping children to stay connected to both sides of their extended families where possible.

The fact that you're reading this now demonstrates your concern about the effect of your divorce on your children. The following summarizes the **findings in the psychological literature**, listed in the parents' bibliography. You are not alone, as about one-half of our children will experience a divorce, about one-fourth will live in a stepfamily, and around 15 percent will experience a second divorce. Professor Constance Ahrons, co-author of *Divorced Families*, and many other researchers discovered that the divorce is not the issue. What matters for kids is how the parents handle the divorce, such as respecting children's right to have two parents.

The research is shifted from family structure (single parent) to process (quality of parenting). A summary of the research is that children experience a crisis period for around two years after the divorce, with boys usually experiencing more difficulty in the shorterm. Children in single parent homes and stepfamilies are slightly more likely to have behavior and academic problems than children in an intact family. The majority of children of divorce are normal rather than disturbed, although "media reports leave the casual reader with that [negative] impression." The differences between children with divorced parents and children in intact families are "statistically significant, but generally quite small," points out Joan Kelly (1993). Studies do not agree about which age is least affected by divorce, but the children of divorce in this book felt it was easier if they were too young to remember the divorce.

An analysis by professors Paul Amato and Bruce Keith of 92 studies comparing children with divorced parents and children with parents in intact marriages (involving over 13,000 children) shows many contradictions. Some studies find long-lasting, negative consequences, while others suggest that most children recover from divorce with few negative consequences. **Higher quality and more recent studies are less likely to show negative effects of divorce.**

Professor Andrew Cherlin estimates that 20 to 25 percent of children will have behavior problems after the crisis period of divorce, compared to about one-half that percent of children living in intact homes. The impact of the divorce depends on the child's age, gender, temperament, number of siblings, and the quality of parenting they receive. A part of the problem is the financial strain that often accompanies single parents.

Amato's review of the studies of adult children of divorce found lasting consequences, such as higher rates of adult depression and divorce, and lower self-esteem. These effects were less likely for well-educated and married adult children of divorce. Booth and Edwards found, though, that remaining in an unhappy marriage has worse effects for the children than divorce. We should remember that these adults experienced the divorce of their parents in an era when it was less common and there were fewer support systems.

~~~

Regarding **gender**, two studies found that boys tend to do better than their sisters in father-custody homes, and girls tend to do better than their brothers in mother-custody homes. (Another study did not find this custody effect for boys.) Hetherington found that single mothers have a harder time parenting their sons than their daughters. She studied children in different family types and categorized them as winners, losers, and survivors. Children of divorce were overrepresented in the first two groups: Girls were the majority of the first group and boys were three times more likely to be in the second group.

Girls are more likely to withdraw, and boys to act out. Girls may exhibit a "sleeper effect" of the divorce, that emerges in their adolescent dating relationships with boys. They are more likely to date and engage in sexual relations earlier than girls living with two parents. Judith Wallerstein found that by young adulthood, about two-thirds of the girls she followed had difficulty forming lasting relationships, "wary of commitment and fearful of betrayal." They were more likely than the boys to appear "troubled and drifting," although the boys often held themselves back from relationships and were lonely.

Children resume their normal developmental path, **if** they have the loving support, clear limits and routines established by at least one parent, and **if** protected from feeling caught in the conflict between their parents. The main source of disagreement between parents after divorce is criticizing the other parent for being too lenient.

The long-term well-being of the children followed by Wallerstein (California), Hetherington (Virginia), Guidubaldi (38 states), depends on the quality of their relationships with their parents and stepparents. Children have fewer behavior problems when their parents are able to cooperate in childrearing and when the children have **close relationships with both their parents.** Children report that the main negative effect of the divorce is the loss of contact with a parent. Children with a close relationship with their father have higher self-esteem, better school performance, and lower levels of anxiety (Kelly, 1993).

The typical plan is the children see their father every other weekend and one week night (Kelly, 1993). Some studies show that kids do better in cooperative dual-residence arrangements than in sole physical custody arrangements (Kelly, 1993; Maccoby, et al.; 1993) and some find no correlation with the custody arrangement (Kline, et al.). Maccoby et al., also found that mothers were more satisfied with dual-residences than mothers with primary physical custody. The least satisfied parents were sole-custody women whose children had no contact with their fathers.

Some studies show that children's well-being is higher when they have frequent contact with their noncustodial parent and other studies didn't find this effect. It depends on the degree of conflict between the parents and on their parenting ability. Fathers of sons are more likely to stay involved with their children after divorce, as are fathers who are encouraged to stay in contact by their ex-wives, those who have joint physical custody, and those who live nearby. Many fathers blossom when given responsibility for the care of their children, with positive consequences for their well-being.

Organizations to Assist Noncustodial Parents

Mothers Without Custody can be reached by phoning (800) 457-6962.

Divorced father Gordon Clay suggests that fathers who need information on custody issues and parenting after divorce contact the Children's Rights Council (202) 547-6227 or the National Congress for Men and Children (202) 328-4377, both in Washington, D.C., and that they read the "Full-Time Dad" newsletter (P.O. Box 577-N, Cumberland, ME, 04021), and his newsletter, "Men's Stuff", P.O. Box 800, San Anselmo, CA 94979). He has a bibliography about fathers and divorce and resource lists of useful organizations for fathers.

Research indicates that the main reason that fathers disengage from their children after divorce is to escape from power struggles and arguments with their ex-wives and the pain of being a visitor, rather than a regular parent (Ahrons and Miller, 1993).

On the **positive side**, children of single parents are likely to have particularly good relationships with their mothers. Longitudinal studies generally find that children do better with the passage of time after the divorce. Adolescents in single-parent families are likely to be more mature, less traditional in their gender roles, more empathic, have a greater sense of the importance of wisely choosing a spouse, and have a greater sense of their own power than children in two-parent families (Gately and Schwebel). Demo and Acock found that the mother's education level has a stronger effect on the child's school performance than whether the child's parents are divorced.

Twenty-one of the studies examined by Amato and Keith include data on children in **stepfamilies**. They find that these children have about the same problems as children in divorced, single-parent families and significantly more problems than children in intact families. Boys often adapt better to having a stepfather and their well-being is enhanced. In contrast, girls' well-being is not affected or decreases, probably because they have less time with their mothers than when they were in a single-parent family. These gender differences disappear in adolescence, according to Hetherington's observations.

A collection of studies analyzed in Furstenberg's *Remarriage and Stepparenting* found that children do better when their stepfather doesn't immediately jump in as the disciplinarian and gradually provides authoritative parenting (setting clear limits and consequences in consultation with the child, rather than being permissive or authoritarian). Children have an easier time adjusting to a stepfather in a mother custody home than a stepmother in a father custody home. Furstenberg's studies indicate that a majority of stepparents and their stepchildren have fairly or very positive relationships, though more distant than the relationships of biological parents.

The National Survey of Children reports that over one-third of children in stepfamilies experience another divorce. This follows from the fact that the divorce rate is higher for second marriages, especially those with stepchildren. This information indicates the need for counseling with an expert on stepfamily issues and reading about stepfamily dynamics.

The research clearly indicates that what you can do to enhance your children's well-being is to end conflict with their other parent, or at least keep the children out of the crossfire and not use them as messengers or spies. Avoid the situation described by a 21-year-old:

"My parents got divorced eight years ago and I am still caught in the middle and affected by it. How do you tell a kid to get prepared for years of hell?" Learn to cooperate with the other parent like a business partner, always focus on the best interests of the children, and provide authoritative and supportive parenting. Use the services of a mediator to minimize conflict during the divorce.

Children interviewed for *50/50 Parenting* agree with the adult experts that permissive and authoritarian parenting are ineffective. Children want to be consulted on family rules and the consequences for breaking them. They need to know that once limits are agreed upon, they will be enforced. Children need a positive relationship with both parents, so focus on their best interests, even if you would rather that their other parent disappeared from your life.

The youths are divided about the usefulness of adult **counselors**. Peer support groups can be a better answer, partly because they solve the problem of feeling isolated and being unable to share feelings for fear of upsetting parents. As one young person reported, "I feel like I'm the only one. It's kind of weird, but hardly anyone I know has divorced parents." I urge you to see if your school district offers these support groups headed by a trained adult facilitator, as they do in Irvine, CA (Stages); Holland, MI; and Del Mar, NY (Banana Splits), or run by a nonprofit group in San Francisco (Kids' Turn). If not, urge school administrators to begin these groups, which studies show succeed in helping children cope (see Pedro-Carroll and Cohen). Curriculum and training are available for purchase, as listed on page 137.

My last word to parents is to quote the former mayor of Minneapolis, Don Fraser. While in office he realized that families are like flowers that need good soil to flourish and that children should be central to any city policy. For families, the soil is the neighborhood.

Minneapolis, therefore, has developed model programs for neighborhood organizing and planning for the future, as well as the neighborhood watch and block parent programs you might have in your area. After much thinking about our families and doing research for my book *Empowering Parents*, I believe that neighborhood organizing is the best solution for social support.

> The National League of Cities is a resource (1301 Pennsylvania Ave. N.W., Washington, D.C. 20004), as is the Minneapolis Youth Coordinating Board (220 City Hall, Minneapolis, MN 55415), or the booklet "Communities that Care: A Guide for Developing Services for Children," available from the Hogg Foundation (University of Texas, Austin, TX, 78713-7998).

I wish you the best as you proceed with the best interest of your children close to your heart. They'll do fine with your continued love, nurturance, and setting clear limits.

Conclusion

Divorce is not something anyone plans on or desires, yet it happens to about one million children under 18 each year. With the help of a skilled mediator or counselor, parents and children can figure out a fair arrangement of shared parenting where kids have close contact with both their mother and their father.

Just as steel has to go through a furnace to be purified and become strong, so do humans need to experience difficulty in order to grow and strengthen their weak points. Learning how to survive a divorce can lead to greater self-reliance, enhanced communication and assertiveness techniques, and insight into how relationships work.

Most importantly, our youthful experts advise that you not blame yourself for your parents' divorce and that you talk about your feelings and what you need to thrive as a young person. Most report that the divorce was for the best, although it didn't seem like it during the crisis period. Think about a plan to develop your unique talents and find adults to help you. A support group of your peers, talking about your feelings, and writing in a journal are very beneficial. I wish you well as you find your own path and develop your strengths. I look forward to hearing from you.

Legal Terms

(These terms are still used in psychological writing, but the legal system uses various terms in different states. For example, Washington refers to residential and nonresidential parents rather than custodial parents.)

§ **Custody.** The court-ordered plan of sharing each parent's time with the children. It frequently includes issues such as holiday visitation, health care, expenses, life insurance, education, and relocation out of the county of residence. It may also provide for grandparents' visitation. In some states the time sharing percentages are quantified, such as 60 percent and 40 percent, in order to compute child support payments.

§ **Physical Custody.** This involves the actual placement of the child with one parent (sole custody), or with both parents on a shared time schedule (joint custody). (California was the first state to encourage joint custody arrangements when, in 1979, it asked judges to favor joint custody when both parents request it.)

§ **Legal custody.** This is a separate issue from physical custody. Often the parents will be given joint legal custody, regarding shared decision making about education, religion, recreation, and health. When the parents cannot get along, the courts may place one parent as sole legal custodian to make decisions on his or her own about school, religion, recreation, health care and the like. The most typical arrangement seems to be joint legal custody with physical custody to the mother, especially when the children are young.

§ **Joint physical custody.** Both parents provide a home for the child for a large part of the time, up to one-half each, and they work together on scheduling. They usually also have joint legal custody but not necessarily.

✥ **Sole legal and physical custody**. The child lives with one parent, who has the main say about the child's upbringing, and the child visits the other one.

✥ **Custodial parent**. The parent the child lives with most of the time and who has physical custody.

✥ **Contempt of court**. This occurs when a judge determines a parent deliberately violates the custody or divorce agreements.

✥ **Mediator.** A neutral person who may be referred by the court in the case of disputes. He or she helps the parents to communicate, understand each other's needs, explore their options, and reach an agreement based on mutual needs. Ideally, the mediator is trained as a counselor. Studies find that mediators do cut down on conflict.

Some states appoint a "law guardian," a lawyer to advocate for the child, or employ "Friends of the Court" to mediate and help families follow through with the divorce settlement.

✥ **Spousal support**. Money paid by the parent with more ability to pay to help the financially needy parent gain independence. A time limit is likely for shorter marriages.

✥ **Child support.** Money paid by one parent to the other based on court determination of their earnings, to assist the recipient with child-related expenses. The payer usually has no say on how the money is spent by the other parent.

Questions to Spark Journal Entries

These questions are intended to help define your values, strengths, plans, and the influences on your decisions.

(Thanks to Dr. Jacqueline Sheehan for her additions.)

<u>Me, myself, and I.</u>

📖 What are you feeling now?

📖 List five qualities you like about your mind, spirit, and personality.

📖 List five things you like about your body.

📖 What are your greatest strengths and abilities?

📖 What's unique about you?

📖 If you were to become an animal, which one would you pick?

📖 When are you happiest?

📖 When have you laughed the hardest and longest?

📖 Describe your peak experiences when you were at your best and life was most thrilling.

📖 Thinking of your life as a novel, what are the themes?

📖 What secret parts of yourself do people not know about?

<u>Influences on my decisions</u>

✒ Make a life line with your date of birth on the left side and your present age on the right side. Write in the major influences on you above the age when they happened, such as your kindergarten teacher above age five.

✒ In what ways are you like your mother? Your father? Your brothers and sisters (if you have them)?

What does your family expect you to become? Do you agree?

What would you like to do the same or differently from your parents?

How do you think you would be different if you had been born the other sex? How differently would your parents, teachers, and friends have treated you? Would your career goal be different?

If you had a choice, what sex would you be? If you could spend half your life as a female and half as a male, would you do it?

Who are your heroes, your favorite role-models? (They can be people you don't know.)

My values

What do you value most?

Is there any cause you would be willing to die for?

If your home burned down, what things would you take out first?

If an alien from another galaxy asked you to explain the purpose of human existence, how would you answer?

What is the purpose of your life?

Do you think there is an afterlife?

How do you define God?

Do you agree or disagree that you are in charge of your life? If not, who or what is in charge?

In what ways do males have a tough time in this society? Females?

How do you define feminism? What is your position on feminism?

What political party is closest to your political views?

What do you think about the use of drugs, including alcohol and tobacco?

➤ What's your position about sex before marriage?

My relationships

❧ What do you most like about your best friends?

❧ Make a list of the people you've been attracted to, including people you've never met. Are there common traits?

❧ Describe your ideal life partner.

❧ What's the main lesson you have learned from your parents' divorce?

My future

ƒ What are you most looking forward to in the next week? Next month? Next year? Next five years? In your life?

ƒ What are your goals for the next year? The next five years?

ƒ What kind of career do you think would be most satisfying, rewarding, helpful, and interesting to you?

ƒ Describe the ideal family for you when you're an adult.

ƒ At the end of your life, what would you like people to remember about you?

This is the questionnaire completed by our experts. You might want to answer it before you read the summary in the following section.

Questions for People 18 to 25 whose Parents Divorced

I am collecting advice from young adults whose parents divorced to pass on to children currently experiencing divorce. If completing this survey brings up some unresolved feelings, this might be a good time to make an appointment with a counselor.

1. Your age____.
2. The age of your sisters ____and brothers_____.
3. Are you female____ or male___?
4. How old were you when your parents separated (when one moved out) _____?
5. Overall, in school, are you an A B C D student? (Circle one)
6. Name three of your qualities that you're especially proud about.
7. How did your parents explain to you why they were divorcing?
8. Looking back, why do you think your parents divorced?
9. How did you feel at the time when your parents first separated and how do you feel about their separation now?
10. What advice would you give to children whose parents are separating?
11. What helped you to get through the separation? (Other family members? Friends? Counselors?)
12. Since the separation, what is your family's plan for parents spending time with the children? That is, how often do you stay at your dad's home and how often do you stay at your mom's home?

13. Did you get more or less time with each parent after their divorce? How do you feel about this?

14. How much say did you have in making this plan for who sees whom when and how good a plan do you think it was?

15. What advice would you offer to kids who go back and forth between two homes?

16. How has your life changed since your parents divorced?

17. How did you feel when your parents started dating other people after the divorce?

18. If either of your parents has re-married, please describe what it is like to be in a stepfamily and what advice you have for kids who are about to become stepchildren.

19. How do you feel about marriage in your future? If you plan to get married, what will you do to prevent getting divorced yourself?

20. What other advice do you have for kids whose parents are getting a divorce?

Summary of the 268 Questionnaires

Total female: 158 Total male: 110 (The most common response is in the parentheses)

Age when filled out questionnaire (majority in early 20s)
9-5, 10-4, 11-1, 12-5, 13-4, 14-4, 15-6, 16-4, 17-9, 18-19, 19-13, 20-31, 21-47, 22-41, 23-24, 24-20, 25-20, 26+-11

Age at time of divorce (majority were 9 or younger)
1-11, 2-22, 3-17, 4-18, 5-18, 6-14, 7-18, 8-14, 9-13, 10-14, 11-11, 12-17, 13-13, 14-9, 15-13, 16-16, 17-4, 18-5, 19-4, 20-7, 21-4, 22-2

Are you an A, B, C, or D student? (majority are B or better)
A: 37 f, 17 m
A/B: 6 f, 5 m
B: 74 f, 45 m
B/C: 14 f, 8 m
C: 26 f, 19 m
D: 1 f, 3 m

Give positive adjectives to describe self (large majority gave 3 positive responses)
3: 129 f, 92 m
2: 18 f, 3 m
1: 5 f, 5 m
0: 7 f, 3 m

How parents explained the separation (a minority of both parents explained the divorce together to the child)

Didn't or vague: 39

Said not in love or getting along: 30

Don't remember: 18

Both explained: 19

Just said Dad is moving out: 11

Mom explained: 8

Dad explained: 2

Youth's explanation of reasons for the divorce (father to blame or they were both too different and didn't get along) (some gave more than one answer for this and following questions)

Father to blame: 71

  cheated-18

  jackass, mean, selfish, domineering-13

  alcoholic-12

  workaholic-8

  not committed: 9

  other: 6

  violent-5

Too different, opposite: 30

Didn't get along: 27

Married too young: 19

Fell out of love: 13

Mother to blame: 11

  cheated-6

  not happy, married for financial security, doesn't cater to a man's pride, got bad advice, mean-5

Didn't communicate well: 8

Financial problems: 5

Didn't spend enough time together or make enough effort: 4

Us kids: 1

How feel during the divorce (large majority felt badly)

<u>Bad</u>: 135

  hurt, upset-40

  sad-42

  angry-32

  deserted, betrayed, scared-11

  felt responsible-10

Glad, for the better, or didn't mind: 37

Didn't understand, surprised, confused: 23

Don't remember: 19

Missed Dad: 6, Missed Mom: 2

Shut self off from both parents: 2

Sources of help (friends were #1)

<u>Friends</u>: 95

Relatives other than immediate family: 55

Siblings: 46

Both parents: 38

Myself: 37

Counselors: 25

Mom: 21

Staying active: 8

Alcohol: 6

God, religion: 6

Teachers: 4

Pets: 4

Dad: 3
Neighbor: 1

Custody arrangement (the majority were in mother-custody homes and saw their father less often)

All or mainly with mother: 104 (some started out seeing Dad regularly, then this contact stopped or became rare for 19 girls and 9 boys)

See father every other weekend and Wednesdays, alternate holidays: 51 (6 of these see their father every weekend)

Live mainly with father: 41 (one of these lives with stepfather, 12 first lived mainly with their mother then switched)

Equal time with parents (such as alternating weeks): 32

Live with grandparents: 2
(14 young adults live with neither parent)

How much say did you have in the custody arrangement?
(None was the most frequent response) (This usually depends on the age of the child and many changed the arrangement as they got older.)
None: 104
All: 65
Some: 23

Coping Advice (don't blame yourself)
Don't blame yourself: 139

Don't take sides, talk to both parents: 65

Talk to your parents about your needs and feelings: 46

Know that things will get better, it's for the best: 40

Remember your parents still love you: 35

Learn from their mistakes, make the best of a hard situation, think positive, they'll be happier: 32

Keep busy, set goals, focus on your growth: 17

It's hard for your parents, give them support: 15

Talk to friends: 14

Don't try to change them or get them back together: 13

Go to a counselor: 9

Don't try to run away from the problems: 3

Effect of divorce on you (140 positive or neutral, 89 negative)

More responsible, mature, independent: 55

Too young at the time to see a difference: 40

Relationship with father suffered: 16

More cautious and less trusting about relationships: 15

Miss whole family: 15

Life is harder, less happy: 14

Better understanding of relationships: 12

Less money: 11

Get two of everything, including holidays: 10

Life is happier: 9

Miss mom: 9

More insecure, repressed, screwed up: 9

Less tension: 8

Parents are happier: 4

Have a wonderful stepparent: 4

More freedom, more rebellious: 2

Moved: 2
Move back and forth: 1

Advice for going back and forth (stay neutral)
Stay neutral: 30 (don't favor one over the other, don't compare)
Talk about what you want: 18
Have your own room and things at each house: 11
Enjoy and make the best of your time with each parent: 16
Enjoy the luxury of two of everything: 7
Be understanding of your parents, they may be confused too: 3
Get a good counselor: 1
Stay grounded among all the confusion: 1
Gets easier: 1

Reactions to parents' dating (the large majority found it difficult) and remarriage (about evenly divided)
Upset: 62
Fine: 65 (some liked one parent's dates, but not the other parent's)
Resentful, jealous: 37
Didn't like dad's girlfriend(s): 22
Didn't like mom's boyfriend(s): 20
Didn't like it at first, got used to it: 1
Note: Some people were happy about one parent dating and unhappy about the other one, and often upset when a parent immediately started dating.

Stepfather nice: 19
Don't get along with stepfather: 15
Don't get along with stepmother: 13
Stepmother cool, nice: 12
Love or like both stepparents: 4

Advice for stepfamilies (appreciate the advantages)

Appreciate having <u>more family and friends</u>: 20

It gets easier with time, be patient: 13

It's a hard or miserable experience: 10

Give stepparents a chance: 7

Try and get along, be nice: 4

Speak up about your needs: 3

Don't compare yourself to your stepsiblings: 3

If your parents are happier, it's easier for you: 2

Plans for the future (plan to wait and then work hard at being married)

<u>Most plan to marry</u> (with the exception of Maybe-5 and No-15)

Plans for a successful marriage:

  <u>Communicate honestly</u>, work out problems-64

  Wait until ready-34

  Learn from parents' mistakes-16

  Have a long courtship-15

  Marry best friend, same goals-15

  Work hard, be committed-14

  Get counseling-12

  Avoid alcoholic, violent, cheating person-8

  Keep close to God-1

Curriculum for Children's Support Groups

(If you know of others, please inform me.)

Banana Splits (Developed by Elizabeth McGonagle, Wood Road School, Ballston Spa, NY 12020.)
Manual available from Interact in Lakeside, CA, (800) 359-0961.
A guide for facilitators, a volunteer school-based program based on the ideas that kids can help each other cope with the issues they bring up for group discussion.

Children of Divorce Intervention Program, Primary Mental Health Project, Dr. JoAnne Pedro-Carroll, Department of Psychology, Univ. of Rochester, 575 Mt. Hope Ave., Rochester, NY 14620.
Three manuals for group facilitators, for kindergarteners and 1st graders, 2nd and 3rd graders, and 4th-6th graders, including a board game.

Dr. Neil Kalter, Family Styles Project, University of Michigan, 527 E. Liberty St., Suite 203, Ann Arbor, MI 48104.
Three modules for group leaders, for grades 1-3, 4-6, and 7-9, based on the "temporal unfolding" beginning with predivorce conflict to stepfamily issues. Includes ideas for activities such as letter-writing, storytelling, puppet play for younger children, play-writing, and role-playing.

Kids' Turn, P.O. Box 192242, San Francisco, CA 94119.
Six-week educational, rather than therapeutic, groups for both parents and kids, taught by teachers and therapists. Curriculum not yet available for purchase, may be in the future. Activity based (art, newsletter creation, role-playing, etc.)

Rainbows for Children, 1111 Tower Rd, Schaumburg, IL 60173. (708) 310-1880. Developed by Suzy Yehl Marta.
This program includes training and ongoing support for groups of five children, as well as purchase of the curriculum, including facilitator manual and storybooks, games, and other children's activities. Over 400 directors are available to provide facilitator training for schools, churches, etc.

Shapes: Families of Today, A Curriculum Guide on Today's Changing Families for Children Ages Eight to Eighteen, Families in Transition Project, Stepfamily Association of America, P.O. Box 91233, Santa Barbara, CA 93190-1233.
A four-meeting curriculum guide for teachers and counselors, including handouts for students, one for elementary students and one for teens. (Contact the Stepfamily Association for additional bibliography.)

Stages, Guidance Projects, Irvine Unified School District, 5050 Barranca Parkway, Irvine, CA 92714.
A school-based program for children dealing with transitions, including divorce, death, and moves. A curriculum is available for kindergarteners through 6th graders, and for 7th-12th graders (available in Spanish), along with student workbooks, a video, audio relaxation exercise song tape, a play script, and a handbook for training parents and staff. A one-day training at your site is available. This is a pull-out program in Irvine, mainly for elementary school children referred by their teachers. Based on the stages of grieving (denial, anger, bargaining, acceptance, hope).

Chris Summerell and Mary Haezebrouck, $16 check to Chris

Summerell, 2991 Winter Park Rd, Rochester Hills, MI 48309.
A duplicable manual for 8-9 sessions, including student
worksheets. Based on a school pull-out program in an intermediate
school.

National Organizations and Newsletters

Children's Rights Council, (800) 787-KIDS.
220 Eye St. N.E., Suite 230, Washington, D.C. 20002-4362.
Sells books and other information for children and parents, special-
izing in shared custody information. Provides information.

Kids Express, The Therapeutic Newsletter for Kids in Divorce.
P.O. Box 782, Littleton, CO 80160-0782.
A terrific newsletter for elementary school children.

Stepfamily Association of America (800) 735-0329 or (402) 477-
7837, 215 S. Centennial Mall, #212, Lincoln, Nebraska, 68508.
Provides education and support through local chapters and sells
books, videos, and tapes. Write for the catalogue.

Additional Readings for Kids

(Books for young children are included in case you have little sisters and brothers) These are collected from various lists of recommended books.

Ancona, George. *I Feel: A Picture Book of Emotions*. NY: J. Messner, 1977.

Berger, Terry. *How Does It Feel When Your Parents Get Divorced?* NY, 1976.

Berman, Claire. *What Am I Doing in a Stepfamily?* Secaucus, NJ: Lyle Stuart, 1982.

Bienenfeld, Florence. *My Mom and Dad Are Getting a Divorce*. St. Paul, MN: EMC Corp., 1980.

Blue, Rose Watts. *A Month of Sundays*. NY: F. Watts, 1972.

Blume, Judy. *It's Not the End of the World*. NY: Bradbury Press, 1972.

Boegehold, Betty. *Daddy Doesn't Live Here Anymore*. NY: Golden Books, Webster, 1985.

Booher, Dianna. *Coping When Your Family Falls Apart*. NY: Messner, 1979.

Boyd, Lizi. *The Not So Wicked Stepmother*. NY: Viking, 1987.

Brogan, J. and W. Maiden. *The Kids' Guide to Divorce*. NY: Fawcett, 1986.

Brown, Laurene Krasyn and Marc Brown. *Dinosaurs Divorce: A Guide to Changing Families*. Boston: Little Brown, 1986.

Cann, Alison. *Talking About Divorce*. Boston: Beacon, 1975.

Crary, Elizabeth. *Mommy Don't Go: A Children's Problem Solving Book*. Seattle: Parenting Press, 1986 (P.O. Box 75267, Seattle, WA 98125).

Eber, Christine, E. *Just Mommy and Me*. Chapel Hill, NC: Lollipop Power, 1975.

Evans, M.D. *This is Me and My Single Parent: A Discovery Workshop for Children and Single Parents*. NY: Magination Press, 1989.

Evans, M. D. *This is Me and My Two Families*. P.O. Box 31342, Saddle Creek Station, Omaha, NA 68131 (workbook).

Gardner, Richard. *The Boys and Girls Book About Divorce*. NY: Aronson, 1983.

Gardner, Richard. *The Boys and Girls Book About Step Families*. NY: Bantam, 1982.

Getzof, Ann and Carolyn McClenahan. *Stepkids: A Survival Guide for Teenagers in Stepfamilies*. NY: Walker, 1985.

Grollman, Earl. *Talking About Divorce and Separation, a Dialogue Between Parent and Child*. Boston: Beacon, 1975.

Hazen, Barbara. *Two Homes to Live in: A Child's Eye View of Divorce*. NY: Human Sciences Press, 1978.

Hogan, Paula. *Will Dad Ever Move Back Home?* Milwaukee, WI: Raintree Children's books, 1980.

Ives, Sally Blakeslie, David Fassler, and Michele Lash. *The Di-*

vorce Workshop: A Guide for Kids and Families. Burlington, VT: Waterfront Books, 1985.

Jasinek, D. and P. Ryan. *A Family Is a Circle of People Who Love You*. Minneapolis, MN: CompCare, 1988.

Jong, Erica. *Megan's Book of Divorce: A Kid's Book for Adults*. NY: New American Library, 1984.

Krementz, Jill. *How It Feels When Parents Divorce*. NY: Alfred Knopf, 1984 (18 accounts by children 8 to 16).

Lebowitz, Marcia. *I Think Divorce Stinks*. Woodbridge, CT: CDC Press, 1989.

LeShan, Eda. *What's Going to Happen to Me?* NY: Four Winds Press, 1978.

Livingston, Myra Cohen. *There Was a Place and Other Poems*. NY: McElderry Books, 1988 (recommended by the founder of Banana Splits).

McGuire, Paula. *Putting It Together: Teenagers Talk about Family Breakup*. NY: Delcorte, 1987 (summarizes 20 experiences).

Perry, Patricia, and Marietta Lynch. *Mommy and Daddy Are Divorced*. NY: Dial Press, 1978.

Phillips, Carolyn. *Our Family Got a Divorce*. Ventura, CA: Regal, 1979.

Prokop, Michael. *Divorce Happens to the Nicest Kids: A Self-Help Book for Kids (3-15) and Adults*. Warren, OH: Alegra House, 1986.

Richards, Arlene, and Willis, Irene. *How to Get It Together When Your Parents Are Coming Apart*. NY: Bantam, 1976.

Roffe, Eric, ed. *The Kids' Book of Divorce: By, For & About Kids*. NY: Vintage Books, 1982 (written by 20 kids in Boston, ages 11 to 14; 14 of them had divorced parents.)

Sanford, Doris. *Please Come Home: A Child's Book About Divorce*. Sisters, OR: Questor, 1985.

Schuchmar, Joan. *Two Places to Sleep*. MN: Carol Rhoda Books, 1979.

Sinberg, Janet. *Divorce Is a Grown Up Problem*. NY: Avon, 1978.

Sinberg, Janet. *Now I Have a Stepparent and It's Kind of Confusing*. NY: Avon, 1979.

Sonneborn, Ruth. *Friday Night Is Papa Night*. NY: Viking Penguin, 1987.

Steele, Danielle. *Martha's New Daddy*. NY: Doubleday, 1989.

Stein, S. *On Divorce: An Open Family Book for Parents and Children Together*. NY: Walker, 1979.

Thomas, Ianthe. *Eliza's Daddy*. NY: Harcourt Brace Jovanovich 1976.

Troyer, Warner. *Divorced Kids*. NY: Harcourt Brace Jovanovich, 1979.

Wright, Betty Ren. *My New Mom and Me*. Milwaukee, WI: Raintree Children's Books, 1981.

Parents' Bibliography: The Effects of Divorce on Children

(an emphasis on reviews of multiple studies)
See the National Council for Children's Rights for additional bibliography of books for children, parents, stepparents, single parents, and reports on custody and other legal issues. Florence Bienenfeld's *Helping Your Child Succeed After Divorce* and Mellinda Blau's *Families Apart* have useful lists of resource organizations.

Adler, Robert. *Sharing the Children: How to Resolve Custody Problems and Get On with Your Life.* Bethesda, MD: Adler & Adler, 1988.

Ahrons, Constance and Richard Miller, "The Effect of the Postdivorce Relationship on Paternal Involvement," *American Orthopsychiatric Association*, Vol. 63, July 1993, pp. 441-450. (See also Ahrons, *The Good Divorce*, Harper Collins.)

Amato, Paul, "Parental Absence During Childhood and Depression in Later Life." *The Sociological Quarterly*, Vol. 32, No. 4, pp. 543-556, 1991.
   Amato and Bruce Keith, "Parental Divorce and the Well-Being of Children: A Meta-Analysis." *Psychological Bulletin*, Vol. 110, No.1, pp. 26-46, 1991.

Arditti, Joyce, "Factors Related to Custody, Visitation, and Child Support for Divorced Fathers," *Journal of Divorce and Remarriage*, Vol. 17, 1992, pp. 23-42.

Arendell, Terry, "After Divorce: Investigations into Father Absence," *Gender and Society*, Vol. 6, No. 4, December 1992, pp. 562-586.

Berman, Claire. *Making It As a Stepparent, New Roles/New Rules.* NY: Perennial, Hunter House 1986.

Bienenfeld, Florence. *Helping Your Child Succeed After Divorce.* Claremont, CA: 1987.

Blau, Melinda. *Families Apart: Ten Keys to Successful Co-Parenting.* NY: G.P. Putnam, 1993.

Bolen, Rosemarie, "Kids Turn: Helping Kids Cope with Divorce," *Family and Conciliation Courts Review*, Vol. 31, April 1993, pp. 249-254.

Booth, Alan, and John Edwards, "Transmission of Marital and Family Quality Over the Generations: The Effect of Parental Divorce and Unhappiness" *Journal of Divorce*, Vol. 13, No. 2, 1989.

Cherlin, Andrew. *Marriage, Divorce, and Remarriage.* Cambridge, MA: Harvard Univ. Press, 1992.

Cohen, Deborah, "A Taste of 'Banana Splits' Consoles Children Feeling Trauma of Divorce," *Education Week*, Vol. VIII, No. 38, June 14, 1989, pp. 19-22.

Cohen, Miriam Galper. *The Joint Custody Handbook*. Philadelphia, PA: Running Press, 1991.

Long-Distance Parenting. NY: New American Library, 1989.

Demo, David, and Alan Acock, "The Impact of Divorce on Children," *Journal of Marriage and the Family*, Vol. 50, August, 1988, pp. 619-648.

Faber, A. and E. Mazlish. *How to Talk so Kids Will Listen and Listen so Kids Will Talk*. NY: Avon, 1980.

Folberg, Jay, ed. *Joint Custody & Shared Parenting*. NY: Guilford Press, 1991.

Gately, David and Andrew Schwebel, "Favorable Outcomes in Children After Parental Divorce," *Journal of Divorce and Remarriage*, 1992.

Grief, Geoffry and Mary Pabst. *Mothers Without Custody*. Lexington, MA: Lexington Books, 1988.

Herman, Stephen. *Parent vs. Parent: How You and Your Child Can Survive the Custody Battle*. NY: Pantheon, 1990.

Hetherington, E. Mavis, "Coping with Family Transitions: Winners, Losers, and Survivors," *Child Development*, Vol. 89, 1989, pp. 1-14.

"An Overview of the Virginia Longitudinal Study of Divorce and Remarriage," *Journal of Family Psychology*, Vol. 7, 1993, pp. 39-56.

"Presidental Address," *Journal of Research on Adolescence*, Vol. 4, 1993, pp. 323-348.

Hetherington and Josephine Arasteh, eds. *Impact of Divorce, Single Parenting, and Stepparenting on Children*. Hillsdale, NJ: Lawrence Erlbaum, 1988.

Hirshey, Gerri, "What Children Wish their Parents Knew, " *Family Circle*, August 9, 1989, pp. 84-87.

Illsley-Clarke, Jean, and Connie Dawson. *Growing Up Again: Parenting Ourselves, Parenting Our Children*. NY: Harper & Row, 1989.

Kalter, Neil. *Growing Up with Divorce: Helping Your Child Avoid Immediate and Later Emotional Problems*. NY: The Free Press, 1990.
   "Long-term Effects of Divorce on Children: A Developmental Vulnerabilty Model," *Journal of Orthopsychiatry*, Vol. 57, No. 4, October, 1987, pp. 587-600.
   "School-Based Developmental Facilitation Groups for Children of Divorce," *Psychotherapy*, Vol. 24, No. 1, Spring, 1987, pp. 90-95.

Kelly, Joan, "Longer-Term Adjustment in Children of Divorce," *Journal of Family Psychology*, Vol. 2, December 1988, pp. 119-140.
   "Current Research on Children's Postdivorce Adjustment," *Family and Conciliation Courts Review*, Vol. 31, January 1993, pp. 29-49.

Kimball, Gayle. *50/50 Parenting*. Chico, CA: Equality Press, 1988.

Kline, Marsha, et al., "Children's Adjustment in Joint and Sole Physical Custody Families," *Developmental Psychology*, Vol. 25, 1989, pp. 430-438.

Lansky, Vicki. *Divorce Book for Parents*. NY: Signet, 1991.

Lauer, Robert, and Jeanette Lauer, "The Long-Term Relational Consequences of Problematic Family Backgrounds" *Family*

Relations, Vol. 40, July 1991, pp. 286-290.

Lehrman, Karen, "Growing Up With Divorce," *Vogue*, May 1993, pp. 184-186.

Levy, David. *The Best Parent is Both Parents*. Norfolk, VA: Hampton Roads, 1993.

Levy, Judith. *Dad Remembers: Memories for My Child*. Harper Collins, NY: 1993 (a workbook).

Maccoby, Eleanor et al., "Postdivorce Roles of Mothers and Fathers in the Lives of Their Children", *Journal of Family Psychology*, Vol. 7, 1993, pp. 24-38.

Meyers, Michael. *Men and Divorce*. NY: Guilford, 1989.

Pedro-Carroll, Joanne and Emory Cowen, "The Children of Divorce Intervention Program," *Advances in Family Intervention, Assessment and Theory*, Vol. 4, 1987, pp 281-307.
  See also *USA Today*, August 13, 1990, p. 2D, and Alpert-Gillis, Pedro-Carroll, and Cowen, "Children of Divorce Intervention Program," *Journal of Consulting and Clinical Psychology*, Vol. 57, pp. 583-587.

Schwartz, Lita Linzer, "Children's Perceptions of Divorce," *The American Journal of Family Therapy*, Vol. 20, No. 4, 1992.

Shaw, Daniel, "The Effects of Divorce on Children's Adjustment," *Behavior Modification*, Vol. 15, October, 1991, pp. 456-485.

Newman, George. *101 Ways to Be a Long Distance Super-Dad*. Blossom Valley Press, 1984 (P.O. Box 4044, Blossom Valley Station, Mt. View, CA 94040).

Pasley, Kay and Marilyn Ihinger-Tallman. *Remarriage and Stepparenting*. NY: Guilford Press, 1987.

Ricci, Isolina. *Mom's House, Dad's House: Making Shared Custody Work*. NY: Macmillan, 1982.

Teyber, Edward. *Helping Children Cope with Divorce*. NY: Lexington, 1992.

Wallerstein, Judith, and Sandra Blakeslee. *Second Chances: Men, Women, & Children a Decade after Divorce*. NY: Ticknor & Fields, 1989.

Kelly, Joan. *Surviving the Breakup: How Parents and Children Cope with Divorce*. NY: Arbor House; 1980

Visher, Emily, and John Visher, *How to Win as a Stepfamily*. NY: Dembner, 1982.

Walter, Glynnis. *Solomon's Children: Exploding The Myths of Divorce*. NY: Arbor House, 1986.

Wall, Jack, "Maintaining the Connection: Parenting as a Noncustodial Father," *Child and Adolescent Social Work Journal*. Vol. 9, No. 5, October 1992, pp 441-456.

Warshak, Richard. *The Custody Revolution: The Father Factor and Motherhood Mystique*. NY: Poseidon, 1992.

Order Form

Send me the following number of copies of:

_____ *How to Survive Your Parents' Divorce: Kids' advice to Kids*, ($9.95 ea.)

_____ *50/50 Parenting*, ($9.95 ea.)

_____ *Everything You Need to Know to Succeed After College*, ($14.95 ea.)

Videos on **Parenting, Men's Changing Roles** and **Dual Earner Families** are available, (each is 30 minutes long and in broadcast quality color). Please write for ordering or more information.

_____ Subtotal
_____ CA residents add 7.25% sales tax
_____ add $2.00 for handling/mailing

Send your check or money order and/or your comments to:

Equality=Press
42 Ranchita Way, Suite 5
Chico, CA 95928

Please send my order to:

Name _____

Address _____

City/State/Zip _____

Phone: _____

THANK YOU VERY MUCH!